THE

GOSPEL

OF THE

KINGDOM

A compelling message
for such a time as this

By Alex Tinson

THE GOSPEL OF THE KINGDOM

By Alex Tinson

Published by GospelRevolution Publishing
Copyright © 2010 by Alex J.Tinson

ISBN No. 978-0-956564-0-2.

www.gospelrevolution.org

Contents

Acknowledgements

I want to thank my wife, Tanya, who has encouraged and supported me in this endeavour. No doubt much of this book would never have been written if you had not been by my side. I love you!

Thanks also go to my wonderful children, Natalie, Ben, Eliza, Darlene and Max, who sacrificed time with Daddy to get this project completed. I hope you realise it was worth it!

For all those who have encouraged me in the faith and ministry: George Hardisty, Ian Squire, Zhivko Tonchev, John Won and Andrew Chan. Plus all those who have impacted my life including all the folk at the Crawley New Life Church.

Special thanks also to those whose editing skills directly helped put this book together, including Andrew Strom and Rob Woolley.

Most of all to my wonderful Saviour who has brought me out of darkness and into His most wonderful light! May this book be the vehicle through which many re-discover their intimacy with and confidence in You. All glory, praise and honour to your Name!

The Gospel of the Kingdom

Preface

Jesus says He will not return until the Gospel of the Kingdom has first been preached throughout the world. This makes it vitally important for us who would claim to represent Him to have a sound grasp of what this message says, yet how many today really know what the Gospel of the Kingdom is all about let alone are actually preaching it?

There may be many who will not want to hear what this book has to say because its words will directly challenge everything they've ever heard, believed or put their faith in. We have to realise that if our beliefs cannot be questioned or challenged in reality they are worth little. The time has come for the real, authentic, life-changing gospel to be proclaimed in an age when the earnest pursuit of God's truth seems to have been thrown out of the window in favour of messages that sooth and tickle people's ears. By God's grace may such a grave charge never be accurately levelled at us.

The Gospel of the Kingdom is a word for such a time as this, when lukewarmness and apathy grip large portions of the church. It is frightening to see so many in the church who are literally sound asleep in their faith yet have not the slightest idea of their perilous state. The Gospel of the Kingdom is a message that will shake you to your foundations and bring a conviction to your Christian walk that has the power to directly affect the world around you. It will blow the spiritual sleep from your eyes and place a compelling drive in you to be ready for our Lord's return and give you an urgency to reach out to others with this very same message. This is a book with depth so be careful to **take the time** to absorb everything within it. And as you read be prepared to encounter the living gospel that Jesus and His apostles preached that turned their world upside down, the gospel which truly is the, "**POWER** of God unto salvation"!

Chapter 1
Why I Asked the Question

We live in a time when there is much emphasis on how we present the gospel, how we can make the Bible message more attractive to those outside our four walls. This seems to be a dominant theme in much of the preaching that goes on in churches and via the Christian media in this day. As far as I'm concerned, I believe it is important to contemporise the gospel and to reach out to those who have not heard the life-changing message of salvation in Jesus Christ. However I also have to ask, once we have overcome all obstacles and managed to reach these people, **exactly what message are we giving them?** Are we reaching them with the same message that Jesus and the apostles brought, or has the heart-piercing, life-changing gospel been altered in some way to one that is more acceptable to the people we seek to reach and perhaps even more worryingly, to those inside the very church we aim to bring these people to?

I remember a time when as the head deacon one Sunday morning I was tasked with organising the whole set-up for our church's morning meetings. I had stayed over the night before with friends who lived close to the church, so that I could make sure I was there before anybody else. Arriving early I unlocked the container and as the set-up team arrived, began the long process of setting up the chairs, platform, sound-system, instruments, front carpet, biscuits, teas, coffees, book-stand, welcome packs, toys for crèche, activities for the youngsters, offering buckets, recording and projection equipment and whatever else was necessary for the smooth running of the two morning services.

We had no building of our own so were meeting in a function room of the Harlequins Rugby club based in South-West London.

Due to the scale of the set-up and time constraints, we had a team of around 20 to 30 working on this task, all arriving early and co-ordinating their efforts to produce what was ultimately a very slick and professional service. This was five star church in action! The designated quiet room was set aside for the senior minister complete with Lavazza coffee, fresh muffins and attractive flower to allow him peace and serenity in order to prepare for the ministry ahead. Toilets were cleaned and equipped with expensive air fresheners and hand soaps to make people feel spoilt and in the right mood to receive from the service. Attractive 'hospitality' workers were stationed at their posts to make sure any visitor felt personally valued, relaxed and happy to be there. Packages of Ferrero Rocher chocolates were left at strategic places to be given to all visitors, ensuring their time at our church was one they would want to repeat. No expense was spared, no stone left unturned to make a visit to our church something dynamic and invigorating, an experience one would always remember.

Once the two services had been concluded and all had had their fill of fine quality coffee and biscuits, everything was then cleaned up, cleared and eventually packed away. My family had long since left for home so I took the train instead. As there was engineering works, I had to leave the train and finally get a coach home, arriving sometime in the evening. This was supposed to be my day off as I normally worked in our business from Monday to Saturday. At this stage in life I was regularly working 16 hour shifts on a daily basis. Having a young family with five children I did not get much spare time. Yet I was happy to do all this, because I felt I was doing an important work for the Lord.

Due to the pressure of facilitating the services, the counting of the offering, looking after every detail, I had not thought too much of what had actually been preached that morning. All efforts had been targeted and fully engaged in creating a platform from which the senior minister could deliver his catchy message, yet after listening to it later, I was left unmoved. It was full of dynamic stories, quotes from the Bible, rousing speeches and easy to apply psychology, yet it left me spiritually empty inside. The thought struck me, "We have all gone to such great efforts to help people hear from God, to facilitate the message, but was it the Word of the Lord that we were listening to?" Were we actually hearing the gospel? It was a frightening question to ask, and one I did not get the answer to until a few years later. Was this the true gospel that I had been listening to? It certainly had quotes from the Bible and Jesus's name was mentioned regularly but **was it the gospel?**

It was a number of years later that I made the startling discovery that practically everything that was being taught in this church, every major focus in the preaching was the complete **opposite** of what is the true Biblical gospel. I was shaken to my foundations! I decided I could not rest until I had come to understand what this gospel was all about and set my heart to understand it. I had to know what was the message proclaimed by the apostles that brought such conviction to the hearts of those who heard it and made the early church so spiritually dynamic and powerful.

This book is a result of that pursuit. I feel the time has come to clarify exactly what the gospel is all about. What is the message we are supposed to be bringing in this day when the coming of our Lord draws ever closer. Many of you will have never read a book like this. It may well take you out of your comfort zone and put alarming thoughts in your mind. It may cause you to rejoice and increase your longing for the day when the Lord Jesus is revealed from heaven in power and great glory. Whatever its effect on you I pray that it will be the vehicle for a fresh move of God in your life. And if you happen to come across a perspective of the Bible you have never considered before, or that challenges your viewpoint, instead of rejecting it out of hand be careful to first ask yourself these questions:

1. Is this what the Bible is really saying; does the scripture quoted ring true?
2. Do I question what is being said because of an opinion I hold based on what people have told me or what I have read in books other than the Bible?
3. Is the Holy Spirit speaking to me through these words?

4. Does my conscience and spirit witness inside to the things I am reading?

If God is speaking to you, I pray you will have ears to hear and eyes to see, "What the Spirit says to the churches," (Rev.2:7).

Chapter 2
What is the Gospel of the Kingdom?

If you ask most people this question they will probably look at you for a few seconds and then answer something to the effect of, "Well isn't it the good news about Jesus and the Kingdom of God, that we can now go to heaven?" Though in some senses true, such an answer reveals a general ignorance that people have today about what the true gospel actually is. Others may say, "It's something that is inside of us, a Kingdom that must be forcefully advanced by violent men." Still others will suggest that it is all about us taking territories and cities for Jesus, operating in 'Kingdom authority' to such an extent that once we've subdued all enemies the Lord Jesus can return to receive His Kingdom.

People debate whether it is a spiritual or earthly Kingdom, the significance of Jerusalem and Mount Zion, whether these will be literal physical places in the Kingdom or just types and shadows of something else which is to come or perhaps has already come! How about the 1,000 year reign of Christ described in Revelation chapter 20? Is this what the gospel of the Kingdom is pointing to? Does 'the Kingdom' have any relevance to our lives now? What about the Kingdom parables dotted throughout the gospel accounts? Presumably they have a lot to teach us about what Jesus meant by 'the Kingdom' yet if you take them at face value, it's not all that easy to correlate what the parables seem to be suggesting with what many people believe today. Why do we think we can just take these parables in a very general sense because they don't fit with our pre-conceived ideas? Is this how Jesus interpreted His own parables or did He attach importance and weight to every detail mentioned? Why did Jesus say that the gospel of the Kingdom must be preached in the whole world as a testimony to all the nations before He would come again?

What is so important about this particular aspect of the gospel message?

This book is all about answering these questions, of taking the difficult and awkward scriptures we usually skirt around and seeing what the Bible as a whole says on this subject. It is so easy to avoid passages that we don't understand and find difficult to fit with what we think the Bible is saying, but isn't this just putting our faith in only **part** of God's Word? I have found it often takes courage and a leap of faith to face up to what the Bible is really saying, and allow the Holy Spirit to put the jigsaw together and direct our Bible studies rather than the systems, opinions and thoughts of man. So many people today seek to build a doctrine on one or two verses that fit with what their viewpoint of the gospel is, but Psalm 119 and verse 160 says, "The **sum** of Your Word is truth." Every part of God's Word contains truth but only taken together can it be accurately described as 'the truth.' We must marry the awkward passages with the relatively obvious ones in order to arrive at what is the true gospel, the pure gospel that Jesus and all His apostles preached, the only gospel that can truly change the lives of those who hear it. Partial gospels may contain some truth but are in danger of becoming 'another gospel' if they become all we ever focus on. We must look at **all** the passages of scripture that talk about and explain the gospel of the Kingdom before we can truly say we have a handle on this subject. Surely this is one of the most important things we could ever do.

Setting the Scene
In Matthew chapter 24 the Lord Jesus was asked by His disciples when the destruction of the temple would occur and what would be the sign of His coming and the end of the age. He then gave them a long discourse on the signs that would lead up to this climatic event and what His coming would be like to those living in those days. He spoke very pointedly to **His disciples** that **they** should be ready for that day and then gave them four parables to show what would happen to those who heeded His warnings

and those who did not. These are the parables of the faithful and evil slave put over the master's household (Matt.24:45-51), the wise and foolish virgins (Matt.25:1-13), the parable of the talents (Matt.25:14-30) and the parable of the sheep and the goats (Matt.25:31-46). Later in this book we will look at some of these parables in detail.

In the midst of this long discourse Jesus made this very important prediction in Matthew 24 verse 14 that,

> **"This gospel of the kingdom shall be preached in the whole world as a testimony to all the nations, and then the end will come."**

Jesus did not say that the gospel that suits us or the one that brings us the most money, power or influence in the world is the one that we should be preaching. He said specifically that **this** gospel of the Kingdom shall be preached. In other words, the gospel He was focusing on in the Olivet discourse, the one about a King coming to receive His Kingdom and what He would do at His coming was the one that had to be preached in all the world as a testimony to them before the end will come.

One Gospel

There is only one gospel as there is only one faith (Eph.4:5) and it all points to one person who is Jesus Christ. There are not two, three or maybe four gospels out there, there is only one. However, there are different **aspects** of this one gospel, perspectives that perhaps major on or emphasize certain areas. The Bible speaks of 'the gospel' in a number of ways. For example it speaks of the gospel of God (Rom.15:16), the gospel of salvation (Eph.1:13), the gospel of the grace of God (Acts 20:24), the gospel of His Son (Rom.1:9), the gospel of peace (Eph.6:15) and the eternal gospel (Rev.14:6). Trying to compartmentalize all of these into particular aspects and emphasis may be unhelpful as they tend to mean much the same thing. This is the good news of our eternal salvation and peace with God, a salvation which is in His Son and has been brought about by the unmerited grace of our Sovereign God. However there are two distinctive aspects of the gospel spoken about in scripture that seem to have a very definite emphasis and application. Though there is cross-over between them, and they both point to the supremacy of Jesus Christ, they also tend to have their own individual focus. These are the **gospel of Christ** and the **gospel of the Kingdom.** This book is all about the latter.

Aspects of the Gospel

The Israelites were commanded to eat the manna that fell in the wilderness to nourish and see them through safely to the Promised Land (Ex.16:15). The manna was a single entity yet tasted of the 'juices of oil' (Num.11:8) whilst also tasting of the 'wafers of honey' (Ex.16:31). The one gospel we are supposed to be feeding upon is the pure doctrine and words of Jesus Himself, Him who is the Manna that came down from heaven. However a very distinctive flavour to this one gospel is the **gospel of Christ** (Rom.15:19 & Gal.1:7), that perspective of the good news which is revealed through focusing upon the various types and shadows of the Christ found in the Old Testament and how they were fulfilled in Jesus. As we piece them together by inspiration of the Holy Spirit, we understand how the gospel works; indeed you could say that the gospel of Christ **undergirds** and is the **foundation** for the whole gospel in its fullness, as the teaching the apostles gave in the early church was all brought to light through an understanding of Jesus as the Christ of the Old Testament. This may be a weighty subject yet it is essential we get to grips with it if we are to grow up in our salvation. As the early apostles saw Jesus as the Living Manna that fell from heaven, they learnt vital lessons of how they should spiritually feed themselves and the flock under their care and wrote about it in their letters to the churches (I Cor.3:1-2, I Tim.4:6, Heb.5:12-14, I Pet.2:2). Him, Jesus, as our Passover Lamb helps us to understand the process of atonement, forgiveness of sins and salvation. Christ as the Rock that was struck teaches us the sufferings He underwent and the importance of faith in the completed work on the cross. The apostle Paul stated that he received his particular understanding of the gospel through a revelation of Jesus **Christ**, not a revelation given **by** Jesus but a revelation **of Him** as the fulfilment of the Promised One, the Christ presented by the Old Testament scriptures (Gal.1:11-12 - important to read this verse in a Bible version that translates it **literally** such as the New American Standard or the New King James, rather than how it is mistranslated in works such as the New International Version or Good News Bible).

The Foundational Message

The gospel of Christ is mostly found in the letters written by the apostles to the early church and seems the prime way in which the gospel was understood and explained to these early believers. The gospel of Christ should be seen as the foundation of all true Bible teaching and ought to be still viewed in this light today. Too much teaching nowadays is based on the prevailing fashions and the ideas and opinions of man, not on the gospel of Christ. This is a serious mistake to make. We are highly likely to go off on a tangent if we do not base our Bible teaching from an accurate understanding of the Old Testament and how it is fulfilled in Jesus, taking individual accounts and stories from this ancient source and showing how they point to our Lord. This was the focus of teaching in the early church and should still be ours today.

However the gospel of Christ was not usually the way the church **reached out** to the lost, nor the aspect of the gospel they would use in their evangelism, unless of course they were reaching groups like the Jews who were familiar with the Old Testament and could relate to what was being said. Indeed it was not really preached at all unless the people were hungry and wanting to grow up in their faith. It was a gospel preached to eager **disciples**, to help them grow in the grace and knowledge of their Saviour Jesus Christ. It was not thrown before people who were just interested spectators (such as the Epicurean and Stoic philosophers in Athens written about in Acts 17:16-34) or were yet to be convinced of the claims of Jesus. It was not generally put before those who thought they were His disciples but in reality were not at all. We should be wary of where we cast our pearls today. These types of people received a different aspect of the gospel called the **gospel of the Kingdom**.

The gospel of the Kingdom (Matt.24:14, Mark 1:14-15 - literal rendering and NKJV), is that perspective of the gospel that focuses upon the power and authority of the Kingdom rule of Jesus, a power we saw in part in Jesus's life, in that of the early church and today through the anointing of the Holy Spirit, but will see in its **fullness** once Jesus returns and receives the Kingdom. The focus of this gospel is very much the Lord's second coming, what He is going to do at His appearing and how we can prepare ourselves to be ready to inherit this Kingdom once He returns.

The Forerunning Message

Whereas the gospel of Christ is only ever mentioned in the epistles, the gospel of the Kingdom is most apparent in the gospel accounts. It seems to be the prime topic of preaching for Jesus, John the Baptist and the early apostles (Matt.4:17-23, Matt.3:1-3, Matt.10:7) and is the perspective of the gospel our Lord prophesied that **must be preached** in the whole world as a testimony to them **before** He would return in glory (Matt.24:14). As the gospel of Christ can be seen as the foundation of the full gospel, the gospel of the Kingdom should be seen as the **forerunner** to the full gospel, the one that goes **before** other aspects of the gospel. This is so as the one thing the gospel of the Kingdom brings us is the **fear of the Lord,** that essential prerequisite anyone must possess if they are to receive from the Sovereign Lord. John the Baptist preached it to **prepare** the people to receive their Messiah. Jesus and His disciples preached it to **prepare** the masses for His atoning sacrifice on the cross and the outpouring of the Holy Spirit on the day of Pentecost, the birth of the church. If this is how Jesus and all His leaders used it, to **prepare** God's people for Him to move in their midst, we would be well advised to do the same.

In Proverbs 9 and verse 10 we read this:

"The fear of the Lord is the beginning of wisdom."

Before we can receive the wisdom of God, we need to first understand the fear of the Lord. The fear of the Lord prepares our heart for it to be able to receive the wisdom of God. Indeed we will be unable to receive anything of substance from God if we do not first learn the dread of Him. Comfortable Christianity has trouble reconciling concepts such as 'dread' and 'fear' with the Lord as the god many of us have created in the West often seems more like a sugar-daddy in the sky rather than the Lord of heaven and earth who is utterly holy, a consuming fire (Heb.12:29) and who declares with no apology whatsoever,

> **"'Vengeance is Mine, I will repay.' And again, 'The Lord will judge His people.' It is a terrifying thing to fall into the hands of the living God,"** (Heb.10:30-31).

The early church grew up in the fear of the Lord and the comfort of the Holy Spirit (Acts 9:31). The fear of the Lord is **always** the prerequisite for God to move and is perfectly balanced by the comfort of the Holy Spirit. Many today seek the comfort of the Holy Spirit but will never truly find it without discovering the fear of the Lord **first**. The gospel of the Kingdom brings this fear of God into our hearts as it brings us face to face with the awesome reality of the eternal judgement of a Holy God.

The gospel of the Kingdom prepares the heart to be open to God like nothing else can. The parable of the sower shows us clearly that unless the soil of our hearts is deep, well cultivated and free of obstructions, we will not become a fruit bearing believer; it's as simple as that. Far too many people who consider themselves believers today have hearts that are filled up with hardened ground, stones and thorns that are useless to the Master. They are simply unable to hear the life-giving message of the gospel because they cannot receive it. The gospel of the Kingdom is the one thing they need to hear that will cause them to rend their hearts and do business with the Lord Almighty. A hardened heart will never hear what the Spirit is saying to the churches but a broken and contrite heart will. God can do amazing things with a person who will take a hold of the gospel of the Kingdom and who then humbles their heart under His Mighty hand. I am living proof of that!

This Gospel Must be Preached

Jesus said that the gospel of the Kingdom **shall** be preached in the whole world as a testimony to them before the end would come. He did not say that the half-hearted gospel of self that is often put forth as the gospel is the one that shall be preached. No way! He said that **this** gospel, the gospel of **the Kingdom** must be preached before the end will come. The question is, is this the gospel that we are bringing people today, or are we presenting them with something else instead?

Today it would appear there are many who preach the gospel. Certainly many claim to be ministers of Jesus Christ and we now even have our own TV channels so we can spread the gospel around the world. But are we preaching the gospel that the apostles preached, or has it become something else? We appear to be putting more and more time, money and resources than ever into spreading the gospel, but is it the **true** gospel we are reaching people with; could it possibly be that what we consider to be, "The gospel," is actually something else and could it be that what we are putting so much effort into spreading could even be termed in some cases, "Another gospel"? If the apostle Paul were to cast his eye over what is considered to be, "The gospel," today would he agree that it was so? Or would he be so incensed and outraged in spirit over the corruption of the pure gospel he fought so hard to deliver to the people of God in his day that he would cause an almighty confrontation with those who are introducing and encouraging this poison in the body of Christ today? I have no doubt this is what he would do given his position as apostle to the gentiles; as he berated the, "Foolish

Galatians," (Gal.3:1) in his time for being seduced by another gospel I believe he would be even more pointed in his choice of language if he were to ever hear what is presented as the gospel today. And would his words be received by those pushing this new modern gospel, or would he be thrown out from the church for being 'divisive,' 'disturbing the sheep' or 'not flowing with our vision' and probably silenced as fast as is humanly possible?

If we were to carefully go through the New Testament and see what it was that Jesus and His apostles emphasized in their ministry and preaching, if we were honest enough to admit it we would soon realise this is **not** the message many are preaching and ministering today. Jesus and His apostles emphasized **God's holiness**, a **standard of Christian lifestyle** and a **love walk for each other** that few are living up to in these days. Jesus and His apostles majored on preaching that convicted people of sin, righteousness and the coming judgement. Today most people in the Western church have **no concept** they will be judged for anything let alone the possibility that they may one day find themselves cast out of the Kingdom of God. This is an alien thought to them and if you ever dare bring it up you'll be accused of disturbing the flock heaven forbid! The apostles took time to explain and reveal the new way of the Spirit, not the so-called way of the Spirit we see today where followers are encouraged to let themselves go and be free from law (not realising we are now under the law of Christ, or as it is otherwise known, the law of the Spirit - Rom.8:2, I Cor.9:21, Jam.2:12 etc) and to get drunk in the Spirit (it is offensive to even mention these two phrases in the same sentence). The apostles wrote page after page of exhortation and instruction into how believers could, "Walk in a manner worthy of the calling with which you have been called," (Eph.4:1) and how they could truly be a, "New creation," in Christ (II Cor:5:17) not by just saying that they are because they prayed a prayer, joined a church or even got baptised, but by **knowing** how to do so and **applying** the teaching to their lives (I expand this **essential** topic in chapter 9 - "The Normal Christian Life"). How many believers today have **any** working knowledge or understanding of how to, "Gain Christ and…be found in

Him," (Phil.3:8-9) how to, "Put on the Lord Jesus Christ," (Rom.13:14) or even to allow Christ to be formed in them (Gal.4:19), bearing in mind these are phrases related to people **in the church** whom we would consider to be saved, and if saved, wouldn't we consider they already 'have Christ'? Instead of understanding these **essential processes of Christian growth,** we have become adept at, "Having a vision," of, "Taking hold of our inheritance," or even, "Soaking in the Spirit." So many of us have become spiritually dull of hearing and can only receive words that appeal to our flesh. Our Bibles lie open on our tables yet who is hearing in these days, "What the Spirit says to the churches," (Rev.2:7)?

Today there are certainly those who preach **aspects** of the gospel that will have benefit to those listening. Where ministers emphasise God's character, the amazing grace that He has freely given us in Jesus, or encourage believers to lay down their lives for the cause of Christ and His people, they are preaching aspects of the true gospel. However in sections of the church and certainly in the charismatic or Pentecostal style churches I often frequent, I have unfortunately seen what is in reality **another** gospel, become part of the mainstream over the last number of years.

It is my considered opinion that much of what is presented as, "The gospel," today or even the, "Gospel of the Kingdom," is nothing of the kind but is in reality **another gospel** (Gal.1:6), a perversion or twisting of that which is true. No doubt it is called the gospel, the name of Jesus is mentioned regularly and the Bible is often quoted (usually out of context). Yet it is so dangerous for that very fact that because it is called the gospel, Jesus's name is mentioned and some scripture is used to justify it people just accept it as the Biblical gospel. Today the average Christian in the West is painfully ignorant and illiterate in the scriptures. Too often we know so much of what people say about the scriptures, or are grounded in a system of theology someone else has put together, but have not trained ourselves to study the Word of God **independently.** This leaves us wide open for attack from him who is known as the deceiver, Satan our adversary. The one thing he wishes to do more than anything is to pervert the true gospel, because if he can get us to think what we believe is the gospel he has got us exactly where he wants us. He knows all too well that the gospel is, "The power of God for salvation," (Rom.1:16) so if he can get us to believe a false gospel one of two things will happen. Either we will fall away in offence and disillusionment as one day we realise that what we have believed in has no enduring power, or we will fall in the day of trouble as we find our house has been built on sand rather than upon the Rock Christ Jesus (Matt.7:24-27). In either case the result will be the same; we will fall away and his evil work will have been accomplished.

Much of the church in the West and its associated Christian media is indoctrinated by a false gospel that we are now going out of our way to promote to the second and third worlds. So many times I have seen people use this verse in Matt.24:14 which says, "This gospel of the Kingdom shall be preached in the whole world as a testimony to all the nations, and then the end will come," and they say, "We need your money so we can send out people and our books to preach the gospel to the world!" when the gospel they are sending is **nothing like** the true apostolic gospel and certainly completely **alien** to the gospel of the Kingdom they are **supposed** to be bringing. This is a tragedy and is diverting literally millions of pounds, euros and dollars from authentic Christian ministries that could make a difference to so-called ministries that are in reality preaching another gospel. This is a catastrophe!

What Ministries Should we Listen to?
There is a lot of confusion these days with what constitutes a good ministry and what is not. What ministries can we safely feed from and which are best avoided? There are some who preach aspects of the true gospel, but then mix in either large or small doses of error that can have an adverse affect on their hearers. Just picking out and listening to the authentic gospel can have benefit and God can speak to people through these nuggets of truth. God is Sovereign and He can speak through whoever He

likes; He spoke through a false prophet called Balaam in Numbers chapter 23 and 24, through the wicked High Priest Caiaphas in the time of Jesus (John 11:49-52) and even through Balaam's donkey (Num.22:28-30)! I know for a fact that God has spoken to me through people whom I would now consider to be in serious doctrinal error. Through God's grace and mercy He spoke and ministered to me, not through the error they preached but through something good they said. However now I have come to realise that part of their message had gone off-track, I would never deliberately choose to feed from that ministry again; and nor would I encourage others to feed from it either. Who wants to eat a fresh hamburger with gone-off cheese in it if they knew it was gone off? And even more seriously, who would think to eat that hamburger if the meat itself had gone off? The mouldy cheese may give you an upset stomach but the rotten meat may be infested with e-coli and result in a one way trip to the local morgue. Who would choose to eat such food if they knew it was contaminated? Only a crazy person would do such a thing!

If the error concerns a peripheral issue then it may not have such an impact. Like eating some slightly gone-off food it may give you a minor spiritual stomach ache so to speak and that's about it. However if the error concerns the Deity of Christ or one of the foundations of the faith, this ministry becomes dangerous and should be avoided. There is a time to eat the cherries and spit out the pips, but if you're eating an omelette and one of the eggs has gone bad you should avoid it at all costs - don't touch it with a barge pole! Ministries that introduce serious error into their core beliefs that then spread to affect the whole gospel message they present are highly likely to be spiritually lethal. That is like eating spiritual cyanide or anthrax. Don't ever play with such food - spit it out at once and get rid of it!

No doubt some people will think, "You're talking as though all these people have error in their ministries and you don't. How do you know you're right and they are wrong? That's just arrogance!" The thing is if we hold onto and put forward statements like this, nobody will stand up for what is right because truth all of a sudden becomes relative to whoever is articulating what they consider to be the truth! This is a real, "Let's not take a stand on anything in case someone doesn't like what we've said and gets offended at us," type of Christianity that was foreign to the early apostles. They all certainly knew what the truth was and were not shy in letting people know it. However if we look at their lives, they were the ones who personally spent much time with Jesus. They listened to what He had to say and took it to heart, rather than spending their time following other people's opinions of what Jesus was supposed to have said and meant. The apostle Paul said,

> **"Not walking in craftiness or adulterating the word of God but by the manifestation of the truth commending ourselves to every man's conscience in the sight of God,"** (II Cor.4:2).

By striving for the truth over and above what people said was the truth and being bold enough to declare it struck a chord in those who heard the apostle Paul preach. When God's Word is preached in spirit and truth there is a ring of truth to it - it feels right to us. It is **commended to our conscience** and just sits right in our hearts. That is why when I began this book I said if you come across anything in it that you have not previously considered, before discarding what is being said first ask yourself these questions:

1. Is this what the Bible is really saying; does the scripture quoted **ring true**?
2. Do I question what is being said because of an opinion I hold based on what people have told me or what I have read in books other than the Bible?
3. Is the Holy Spirit speaking to me through these words?
4. Does my conscience and spirit witness inside to the things I am reading?

We need to be like the people of Berea in Acts chapter 17 and verse 11 who did not just accept what the apostle Paul himself said at face value just because he was such a respected leader, but went to the scriptures themselves to find out if what he said was true. We need to start studying the Word of God for ourselves so that we may know the truth that truly sets us free. Anything you hear from me in this book be sure to test it out with what the scriptures say first. I do not claim to be the only one who has a handle on the truth; far from it. However I do know something of God and His Word and I invite you to check out what I have discovered by studying it yourself. That which is true will always stand up to scrutiny and genuine examination.

Having said all this, it is a fact that certain ministries do exist which strive to preach the true gospel. I have personally met people who are quietly getting on with the Master's business, teaching and preaching the true Word of God, being rich in good deeds and feeding orphans and widows as we have been commanded to do. There are individuals and ministries that are true who have a desire to preach the original gospel and these **should** and indeed **need** to be supported in order to get the message out - the time is short and we must do His work whilst it is still day, before the night comes when nobody can work (Jn.9:4). However it appears in the West that in the last few years another gospel has become a part of the **mainstream line of thinking** and due to our influential position in the world this particular perversion of the gospel is being successfully exported throughout the body of Christ worldwide. In many cases we are ending up spreading a poisonous, fake gospel all over the world, thinking that we are doing God and His people a favour. We could not be further from the truth if we tried.

I do not have time in this book to run through all the different facets of this fake gospel that has gripped so many in this modern world. People have already spoken and written extensively about such things. Suffice to say that any teaching that emphasizes self, or presents another God or another Jesus other than the one clearly portrayed in scripture is another gospel. Additionally any doctrine that is not according to the six foundations of the faith listed in Hebrews chapter 6 and verses 1 and 2, is another gospel, especially if it encourages doing things to get anything from God and a different type of faith other than the Biblical faith which is in God and accessed through Christ our Lord. In this book I seek to emphasize what is the **true gospel**, the actual message we are supposed to fight for and be bringing to the world in these days. There is a saying that if you can train a bank clerk to become familiar with handling genuine bank notes, when a false one comes along they will be able to spot it immediately. I believe there is need to point out heresy and false teaching in the church. It is imperative that we do this and there are people out there doing a great and important work in this area. However if this is all we do we run the real risk of becoming unbalanced ourselves, always pointing out everyone else's faults whilst steadily growing in arrogance and pride in our own 'enlightenment,' and supposed spiritual superiority. To be honest with you, it is pretty tedious to get around such people for any length of time as their critical spirit gets more and more nauseating. We must be discerners of that which is false yet it is **even more important** to familiarise people with that which is **true**. We need to point out the error but go out of our way to ground people in the true gospel. This is of critical importance and a reason for this book to be written. Once we know and are walking in the light of the true gospel, any other message will be abhorrent to us and we will reject it out of hand because we see how empty and hollow it really is.

As I see what is being preached from so many pulpits today there seems in some quarters to be an emphasis on how we package and present the gospel to the world. I personally believe in contemporising the Christian message and making it relevant to those who hear. If we are speaking to people unfamiliar with the gospel it needs to be presented in an easy to understand manner. People in the West are used to dynamic messages appealing to them from every side and we too need to be modern and professional if we are to get people to even consider the claims of Christ. This is being wise and adapting to the culture we live in for the sake of reaching the people whom Christ died for. The apostle Paul did whatever it took within the constraints of holy living to relate to people on their cultural and sociological level in order to win their attention to the message he was trying to bring them. He said,

> **"I became as a Jew, so that I might win Jews...**
> **To the weak I became weak, that I might win**
> **the weak; I have become all things to all men,**
> **so that I may by all means save some,"**
> (I Cor.9:19-23),

and we should follow his example. However the central message needs to stay the same; we cannot change the central message in order to make people feel comfortable and get them into our churches. This is criminal in God's eyes. The fake gospel that is becoming so prevalent now in our Western churches is so hollow, shallow and lacking in power at its heart that I believe there is getting more and more emphasis on the **presentation** rather than the **message itself** in order to disguise this fact.

Packaging and Presentation

A number of years ago I was in a relatively new church in London that has already become one of the most successful in the UK through its dynamic worship and promotion in the Christian media. The visiting speaker was sharing from Matthew chapter 13 and verses 45 and 46, the parable of the pearl of great price. The whole point of his sermon was that the pearl is so precious that we need to package it the best we can so others can identify it as something of value too. This is what you do with items of high value. The focus of the entire sermon was about the packaging, not really the pearl itself. The obvious inference was that the more money and time you spent on making the pearl look good, the more you were obeying God and doing things that pleased Him. Now is this the message Jesus was trying to give us in this parable? Not at all. No doubt the merchant seeking fine pearls had to look really hard to find this one of such high value. Maybe he had need to travel over land and sea, scouring the markets and shops, doing a thorough research and talking to traders and people in the know before he could acquire it. It is clear from what Jesus said that it was not found in the most obvious of places on public display, beautifully packaged at a fashionable jewellers or the finest boutique in town. No the merchant had to expend much time and effort searching for it as it was in a sense **hidden** and the merchant had to go out of his way to **find it**. The whole point of the parable is the **preciousness of the pearl** and the **effort** required to find it. It has **absolutely nothing** to do with how we package the pearl. If the merchant had found the pearl in a dirty old rag or buried under a pile of earth, what would he care? All he was focused upon was getting the pearl, though it would cost him everything he had, he was willing to do whatever it took to get that pearl. The value was in the pearl not in its packaging. This is a concept presented in the gospel of the Kingdom and we will see it more and more as we go along that to find the Lord Jesus Christ and become one who will inherit the Kingdom will cost you everything you have. Jesus is looking for those who will do **whatever it takes** to truly possess Him and take hold of the coming Kingdom. This is a central theme of the gospel of the Kingdom and one that **must** be preached in the days in which we live. The message of the gospel has nothing to do with how it is presented or packaged. This is a diversion; it is not the gospel itself and should not be the focus of our preaching.

When Jesus said in Matthew chapter 24 and verse 14 that, "**This** gospel of the Kingdom shall be preached," it is clear that the subject matter He was focusing on in Matthew chapters 24 and 25, this particular aspect of the gospel was the message He was meaning that must be preached to all nations as a testimony to them before He would return in glory. This was the gospel of the Kingdom. This is not to say that we ignore the rest of the Bible and just preach these two chapters, far from it! However we will see a theme to these two chapters that clearly brings out what the gospel of the Kingdom is all about, a theme Jesus often referred to, that when understood, helps us to put together much of what the rest of the Bible talks about as well.

In this long sermon recorded in Matthew chapters 24 and 25, Jesus spoke of difficult times ahead, of people's faith being tested and many not passing this test. He speaks with urgency that the time is short and His people must prepare themselves for His coming as a significant proportion of them will be caught unawares and not be ready for Him. From what He says it seems that many people will **assume** everything is just fine until they are called to give account, and then they will find to their horror that they have been **sleeping on the job** and are **unready**. Again He speaks of many being **denied entry** into the Kingdom of God, a Kingdom that rules and dominates the earth in a way that may seem incredible today.

What is This Kingdom?

Throughout the scriptures one of the recurring themes is that of the Kingdom of God. In a hidden mysterious sense, it is revealed as the new creation in our hearts, what any true believer experiences today by the indwelling Holy Spirit. However in its fullness the Kingdom of God is clearly portrayed as something that will be a **physical reality** one day on this earth, as the coming Messiah, God's Shepherd or as He is also known, "My Servant David," (Ez.37:24) rules and reigns from Mount Zion in Jerusalem over the nations of this world. This of course will never happen until the Lord Jesus Christ returns to the earth at His second coming. Our Lord returns in glory and the Kingdom power, influence and authority is brought to bear on the creation and on the peoples of this world. This is what the Biblical concept of, "The Kingdom," is all about in its fullest sense. When John the Baptist, Jesus and His disciples preached, "Repent for the Kingdom of God is at hand," they were telling the people to get themselves ready for the Messiah was coming, the Chosen One who would rule this Kingdom. The King of this Kingdom was soon to arrive or was indeed standing right before them. Since their preaching we have been waiting nearly 2,000 years for this Kingdom to fully materialise. But one day soon it will, and we shall see the Kingdom of God before our very eyes, exactly as it was prophesied all those years ago.

The Kingdom Present and Future

Let me just say that the emphasis of the return of Jesus and the establishment of His rule contained in the gospel of the Kingdom in no way detracts from the fact that we experience His Kingdom to some extent today through the power of the Holy Spirit in supernatural giftings, ministries and graces given to the church (I Cor.12:4-6). The Israelites tasted some of the fruit of the Promised Land whilst still in the wilderness (Num.13:23-27) and we also can taste something of the, "Powers of the coming age," (Heb.6:5) whilst still in the body awaiting our Lord's appearance from heaven. In a **situational sense** we are currently in the wilderness of this world on our way to the Promised Land of Christ's Kingdom that will one day be a physical reality here on earth. Yet in a **spiritual sense** we can enter into this land flowing with milk and honey by the Spirit through faith. In a **spiritual sense** all true believers are currently seated with Christ in heavenly places (Eph.2:6) yet one day this will become a **physical reality** as those who overcome in the wilderness of this life will be given the right to sit down on the throne of Jesus in His Kingdom established for all to see (Rev.3:21). The mistake we tend to make is seeing where we are today as the fullness of this Kingdom which it is not. We can experience **some** of the Kingdom power in our lives today by faith but it is just a **part** of that Kingdom authority that will only be fully unleashed when Jesus returns. Today we can taste of the heavenly manna as the Spirit reveals the mysteries of the scriptures to us. We can operate in some measure of the power of God as the Spirit distributes His gifts as He wills (not as we will as some try and argue - see I Cor.12:11). However this is all in part; **it is the Kingdom coming, not the Kingdom come.**

Today the Kingdom of God reigning in our hearts is a relatively hidden thing, a treasure stored in jars of clay (II Cor.4:7) which relates to our physical bodies. This treasure is observable only on occasion as God's people walk in the power of the Holy Spirit as they exercise faith in Him. Of course we should do all we can to encourage believers to walk in this power as the Spirit leads, to demonstrate something of the treasure we have on the inside to a lost and dying world. We are living in the age when the Spirit has been poured out on all flesh, and we are called to be **filled with His Holy Spirit power** in order to be His witnesses in Jerusalem, in all Judea and Samaria and to the remotest parts of the earth (Acts 1:8). We need to see more of the true power of God flow through consecrated, faith filled believers today! Let us see the authentic power of God unleashed in our day as it was in the book of Acts, not just the counterfeit or pale imitation we so often see today. Instead of people jerking uncontrollably and behaving like animals let us see the blind receiving their sight, the deaf hearing, demons cast out and the dead raised! This is what the early church saw, so much so that they would even bring their sick into the streets for Peter's shadow to touch them so that they could be healed.

However even if we see the power of God unleashed as it was in the early church, this is all, "In part"; we currently know in part, we prophesy in part, and see something of the Kingdom rule in our lives (I Cor.13:9-10). Whatever we are privileged enough to see of the Holy Spirit's power being released in our midst in these days is only a **foretaste** of what will happen when Jesus comes to rule this earth. When He who is perfect, the Lord Jesus returns, the imperfect will disappear and the Kingdom in its fullness will be established for all to see.

What happens with the coming of Jesus is that this one cataclysmic event heralds in the Kingdom of God in its fullness - the nations literally will be ruled with a rod of iron and all things will be in subjection to Him in a way that will never happen until He comes. We are supposed to pray that His Kingdom would come, not thank God that it has already come (Lk.11:2). Today we experience it in part; at the coming of Jesus we will experience it fully as the Kingdom is established, Jesus sits on the throne and all things are placed under His feet. This is what the gospel of the Kingdom is all about and what most of the Kingdom parables allude to, the **coming of the Lord Jesus** and what He is going to do at His coming.

Isn't the Kingdom of God Within Us?

In Luke 17 verses 20 and 21 Jesus said to the Pharisees,

> **"The Kingdom of God is not coming with signs to be observed; nor will they say, 'Look, here it is!' or, 'There it is!' For behold, the Kingdom of God is in your midst."**

Many people today quote this passage as, "The Kingdom of God is within you." This is how it is translated in the New King James and New International Versions of the Bible. I have just quoted it from the New American Standard Bible that renders it as, "The Kingdom of God is in your midst." It appears either version of the phrasing could be considered equally valid.

The point could be made that as Jesus was answering a question posed by the Pharisees He would not have said the Kingdom of God is within you as that would infer that this Kingdom was inside these religious leaders, something that was obviously not the case. By saying the Kingdom of God is in your midst He could well have been referring to Himself as the King of this Kingdom who was standing among them, before their very eyes. As the King of the Kingdom of God Jesus **encapsulated** the Kingdom in Himself, He **represented it**. The Kingdom of God was in their midst as in a sense, He is the Kingdom personified. He would receive it, rule it and populate it only with those who are found, "In Him," at His coming. Much as we describe the philosophy of communism as Marxism due to the huge influence Marx had on its origin and formation, so also Jesus **embodies** the Kingdom of God as it is all about Him from first to last.

It is interesting to note that straight after Jesus said the Kingdom of God was in their midst, He started talking about His glorious second coming, the event which heralds the start of the Kingdom here on this earth. He says His disciples were not to, "Look there! Look here!" (v.23 - very similar phrasing to the previous verses) but to look for the lightening to flash from one end of the sky to the other for this would be the sign of the coming of the Son of

Man. This is the Kingdom in its fullness, the glorious coming of the King who was then standing in their midst.

Unfortunately when a number of people quote this verse today, they do so trying to make the case that the concept of the Kingdom of God is fully realised in the new creation **within** our hearts by the Holy Spirit. In other words, everything Jesus and His apostles taught about the Kingdom is seen in the church today, in the power of the Holy Spirit at work in and through our lives in this hour; they say there is no physical fulfilment of these things, there will be no 1,000 year millennial reign of Christ on this earth.

Personally I find it incredibly difficult to read the scriptures with an open mind and no pre-conceived ideas and arrive at this conclusion. On this point I have to be dogmatic and say there is **no way** you can harmonise the scriptures talking about the Kingdom and hold a view that denies it will be a physical reality one day. It seems patently obvious to me that there will be a physical reign of the Lord Jesus Christ on earth at some point in the future. Yes in a sense the Kingdom is within our hearts today if Christ truly lives in our hearts by faith, but this is the **precursor to the main event**, the coming of the Lord Jesus Christ in power and great glory to establish His Kingdom on earth and,

> **"The summing up of all things in Christ, things in the heavens and things on the earth,"** Eph.1:10.

All true believers today are living stones being built as a spiritual house for a holy priesthood (I Pet.2:5), a house that is to be filled with the glory of God, now in a partial sense but in its fullness at the coming of the Lord Jesus Christ. At His return these living stones are all gathered together to become the, "House of the Lord," on Mount Zion (Is.2:2-4), the living temple in which Christ dwells in splendour and majesty for all to see. This is the Kingdom of God and will be awesome to witness and be a part of.

Chapter 3
The Kingdom Established

During the period between His resurrection and ascension, Jesus spoke many things to His disciples regarding the Kingdom of God (Acts 1:3). This was the focus of His teaching and resulted in His disciples asking Him the question whether He was at that time going to restore the Kingdom to Israel (Acts 1:6). Obviously from what Jesus had been saying and from their understanding of the Hebrew scriptures they expected Jesus at any moment to take up the throne and rule the Kingdom from Jerusalem (Lk.19:11). One of the dominant themes in the Old Testament is the restoration of the Kingdom to Israel, a theocracy led by the Messiah Himself. Now it is true that the Bible is a spiritual book and as such speaks spiritually as well as practically. There is a lot of spiritual truth in the concept of the Kingdom. However reading the scriptures with an unbiased mind would always give the impression that this restoration would be a **physical reality** on earth one day, a material actuality of a spiritual concept. Nobody would logically think otherwise unless they had been taught to think that way by someone who wishes to paint a different picture to that which is plainly seen in God's Word. This was certainly what the Jews of Jesus day thought as did His disciples.

As Jesus made His triumphal entry into Jerusalem stirring up the whole city in the process, the people shouted,

> **"Hosanna!** (Literally meaning, 'Lord save us', presumably from the Romans?) **Blessed is He who comes in the name of the Lord; blessed is the coming Kingdom of our father David; hosanna in the highest!"** Mk.11:9-10.

The common man expected Jesus to go to the temple, be declared the Messiah, kick out the Romans and establish the second golden age of the Jews, following in the footsteps of King David and Solomon. This is what they expected and thought was just about to happen. This was the mindset of most Jewish people at the time of Jesus.

When the angel Gabriel was sent to Mary to announce the incarnation, he said something very significant about the Son she was to bear. He declared that God Himself would give Him the **throne of His father David** (Lk.1:32). The throne of David was synonymous with the Kingly rule in Israel and indeed with the glorious Kingdom that God had promised to the Jews throughout the Old Testament. Whoever occupied the throne of David, ruled the Kingdom.

The Throne of David

Many believers today when asked, "Where is Jesus seated today?" will answer, "On the throne of course!" Technically speaking they are correct, but **which throne** is He currently seated upon? You may not realise it but this is an important point we should all be aware of. In the book of Revelation chapter 3 and verse 21, the Lord Jesus speaking to the church at Laodicea says this:

> **"He who overcomes, I will grant to him to sit down with Me on My throne, as I also overcame and sat down with My Father on His throne."**

So where is Jesus seated at the moment? On His Father's throne. Is this the throne of David? No it is not.

Psalm 110 verses 1 and 2 say this:

> **"The Lord says to my Lord: 'Sit at My right hand until I make Your enemies a footstool for Your feet.' The Lord will stretch forth Your strong sceptre from Zion saying, 'Rule in the midst of Your enemies.'"**

What is the Psalmist saying here? He is saying that when the Christ comes He will sit at the right hand of the Father on His throne, until such time as the Father decides to give Him His own Kingdom complete with His own throne and sceptre. When this great event takes place, all His enemies will be forcefully put under His feet in complete submission to Him. What throne will the Christ inherit at this time? It will be the throne of David. And what of the strong sceptre He will wield in the midst of His enemies? This will be the sceptre of the Davidic monarchy, representing the **overwhelming power and authority** this Kingdom will possess.

Though Jesus has been given all authority and power by His Father due to His triumph on the cross (Matt.28:18), He has not yet begun to exert this power in the way that He will when He sits on the throne of David and His Kingdom is established. As mentioned before, we currently see **something** of this power at work among us through the anointing power of the Holy Spirit. However we do not yet see the **fullness** of this power and authority in our day. When Jesus made this statement to His disciples, He did not then tell them to conquer Kingdoms, battle in the heavenlies and take nations for Him. No, He told them to make **disciples** of all nations, teaching them to **obey** everything He had commanded them.

Jesus did not give them His authority as though He no longer possessed it. This is a crazy doctrine formulated in these days to exalt man rather than our Lord. A government does not give up all its power because it commissions a police force or army to operate in its name. It retains the power and authority and its agents operate **in its name**, utilizing **some** of the power inherent in this name. Jesus said He had been given all power and authority therefore we should go in His Name and make disciples of all nations. He still retains all power, and we will have success as we operate in His Name, and conversely failure if we choose to operate in our own strength or name (even if we tag the name of Jesus to projects begun or run by our own human efforts, as some do today). This includes moving in the power of the Spirit which must always be done as the Spirit leads and not just when we feel like it. Our Sovereign God has no need for us to try and manipulate Him to do what we expect Him to do when we want Him to do it. There is a time to 'press in' but we must always be mindful of whether the Holy Spirit is leading us or if we are just doing our own thing.

Progression of Events

In Psalm 8 we have a prophecy given about the Messiah who was to come and the succession of events that would lead up to Him inheriting the Kingdom. If we read verses 4 to 6 of this Psalm carefully and connect them with what is said about these exact same verses in Hebrews chapter 2 verses 6 to 8, we will see they are talking about a clear **progression of events** that will take place in the life of Jesus. In verses 4 to 6 the Psalmist says:

> **"What is man that You take thought of him and the Son of Man** (a title given to the coming Messiah and adopted by Jesus) **that You care for Him? Yet You have made Him a little lower than God, and You crown Him with glory and majesty! You make Him to rule over the works of Your hands; You have put all things under His feet."**

The Psalmist states there would come a time when people would wonder whether God cared at all for the Son of Man, the coming Messiah. He says, "What is man that You take thought of him and the Son of Man that You care for Him?" During Jesus's ministry on earth people often questioned whether God was really with Him and on the cross many considered Him forsaken of God (Is.53:4). The writer predicts that He would be made a little lower than God Himself, but then would be crowned with glory and majesty. Following this there would be a time when the Messiah is made to rule over the works of God's hands and then finally all things would be put under His feet. This is clearly referring to the time in the future when the Messiah will rule over His Kingdom and all things are placed under His feet in complete submission to Him. The writer of the book of Hebrews takes this very passage of scripture and shows us how this progression of events leading to the establishing of the Kingdom of God on earth, refers to Jesus the true Messiah. In Hebrews chapter 2 verses 6 to 8 the writer lists these verses from Psalm 8. He then shows in verse 9 that Jesus was made a **little lower than the angels** (or 'Elohim'-Ps.8:5) when He emptied Himself and experienced the, "Suffering of death," on a cross. Later at the resurrection and ascension He was **crowned with glory and majesty,** seated at the right hand of His Father where He now awaits the time when He will rule over the works of God's hands and all things will be put under His feet. These last two events have **not yet taken place** but will do so once Christ returns and establishes the Messianic Kingdom here on earth. In verses 8 and 9 of Hebrews chapter 2 it says:

> **"But now we do not yet see all things**
> **subjected to Him** (Jesus). **But we do see Him**
> **who was made for a little while lower than the**
> **angels, namely, Jesus, because of the suffering**
> **of death crowned with glory and honour."**

Presently we have got to the bit which says that God will, "Crown Him with glory and majesty," but have not got any further than this yet. Currently the Kingdom is not established; it is coming but we do not yet see all things in subjection to Him. We cannot establish the Kingdom ourselves. We can proclaim the Kingdom, demonstrate its power to some degree and by God's grace lead people into the Kingdom. However the Kingdom is only established in its fullness once Jesus returns in power and glory. In these days in which we live, we cannot make all the drug dealers stop selling drugs. We cannot enforce integrity in politicians or in executive decisions in high places. However what are we to do? We are to look towards Him who is crowned with glory and honour, seated at the right hand of the Father, pray for righteousness to flourish, shine our light in a crooked and depraved world, rescue all we can from the dominion of darkness and prepare ourselves to be ready for His triumphant return.

The Sign of the Son of Man

When Jesus was speaking to His disciples on the Mount of Olives, He spoke of great signs such as famines, earthquakes, pestilences and wars followed by a severe persecution of His people occurring just before His return in glory. Then in verse 30 of Matthew 24 He speaks of the most important sign they should be looking for, the sign of the Son of Man appearing in the sky. Jesus said,

> **"And then the sign of the Son of Man will appear in the sky, and then all the tribes of the earth will mourn, and they will see the Son of Man coming on the clouds of the sky with power and great glory. And He will send forth His angels with a great trumpet and they will gather together His elect from the four winds, from one end of the sky to the other,"**
> Matt.24:30-31.

As a young believer I wondered what this great sign was. Given that the cross is universally known as the symbol of Christianity, I wondered whether this great sign would be a giant cross suddenly appearing in the sky showing people that it was Jesus returning in glory? I even wondered whether the sign could be a symbol or outline of a great fish such as people have on the backs of their cars to show they are Christians. I didn't really know; I was rather ignorant of these things. Then when reading Daniel chapter 7 verses 13 and 14 it all became very apparent.

> **"I kept looking in the night visions, and behold, with the clouds of heaven One like a Son of Man was coming, and He came up to the Ancient of Days and was presented before Him. And to Him was given dominion, glory and a Kingdom, that all the peoples, nations and men of every language might serve Him. His dominion is an everlasting dominion which will not pass away; and His Kingdom is one which will not be destroyed,"** Dan.7:13-14.

I suddenly realised that the sign of the Son of Man was this great event happening live before all, Jesus the Son of Man Himself appearing on the clouds of heaven in power and great glory, receiving the Kingdom in **full view** of all creation, and not only Him but also the Ancient of Days revealed to the naked eye for the **first time in human history**. Every eye will see Jesus the Christ as He is led before His Father and formally presented with the throne of David and the sceptre of the Kingdom. This is not some hidden event occurring in a small corner of the world. Somehow it will be publically viewed by all who are around in those days. All will see the Father and the Son appearing in the heavens, an event that will be so traumatic and terrifying the sky will be split apart like a scroll being rolled up and every mountain and island will be removed from their places. According to Revelation 6 verses 12 to 17, and also Isaiah 2 verses 19 to 21, the inhabitants of the earth will try and hide themselves in the rocks of these collapsing mountains and will wish for themselves to be crushed by their great weight for such a fate is better than trying to stand before the holiness of the Ancient of Days and His Christ. They say to the mountains and rocks,

> **"Fall on us and hide us from the presence of Him who sits on the throne** (the Father)**, and from the wrath of the Lamb** (Jesus the Christ receiving the Kingdom)**; for the great day of their wrath has come, and who is able to stand?"** Rev.6:16-17.

Once the Lord Jesus receives the Kingdom He sits on His glorious throne, the throne of David and exerts His authority over His church and over the nations.

Chapter 4
The Judgement Seat of Christ

The first thing that happens when Jesus is revealed from heaven is that the antichrist system meant to replace Him and carefully put into place by wicked men will be utterly destroyed. II Thess.2:8 says that the lawless one will be killed with the breath of Jesus's mouth, and brought to an end by the appearance of His coming. The book of Habakkuk chapter 3 and verse 13 details his end even more graphically, appearing to show that he will be carved in two from top to bottom when the Lord Jesus returns!

Secondly at the sound of the trumpet and the voice of the archangel, the resurrection will take place. Daniel chapter 12 and verse 2 says of that resurrection that,

> **"Many of those that sleep in the dust of the earth shall awake, some to everlasting life, some to shame and everlasting contempt,"** (NKJV).

Jesus also says in John 5:28-29:

> **"An hour is coming, in which all who are in the tombs will hear His voice, and will come forth; those who did the good deeds to a resurrection of life, those who committed the evil deeds to a resurrection of judgement."**

Whether Jesus resurrects **all** those who have expressed faith in Him at this point, or just those who maintained their trust in Him **to the end** is not clear. The two scriptures just quoted (and also the parable of the dragnet for that matter) tend towards the former point that all who have begun the journey of faith throughout history will be resurrected at this point whether they finished in the faith or not. However the scriptures found in I Thess.4:16 and Rev.20:4-6 could possibly indicate it will only be those who, "Died in Christ," who will be raised at this point i.e. only those who were faithful to Jesus **when they died** will have a part in this resurrection. The logic of this would then imply that those who **departed** from the faith during their life and then physically died will only be resurrected **after** the 1,000 year reign of Christ, at the Great White Throne judgement (Rev.20:11-15). I personally feel the first point is probably correct, that all who have come to the faith throughout history will be resurrected at the return of Jesus, whether they continued in the faith or not; however I am not sure we can be dogmatic on this issue. Whatever is the case, those who are resurrected at the return of Jesus will all appear before His tribunal, the judgement seat of Christ.

Next, Jesus sends out His angels to gather those still alive, who have expressed faith and joined themselves to Him at some point in their lives. We often call this great event **the rapture**. Those fitting this bill will all be snatched away in the clouds, joining the Lord Jesus as He descends to earth as foretold by the angels in Acts 1:11, coming to sit on the throne of David and rule the nations from Mount Zion. Those who are raptured, are being gathered together for the purpose of appearing before the judgement seat of Christ, as it says in II Cor.5:10-11:

> **"For we must all appear before the judgement seat of Christ, so that each one may be recompensed for his deeds in the body, according to what he has done, whether good or bad. Therefore, knowing the fear (NKJV - 'terror') of the Lord, we persuade men."**

All in the church, who have professed faith in the Lord Jesus Christ will be summoned to appear before the tribunal of Christ; there will be no exceptions. No bribes will be accepted, no preference given; it is the destination for every person who has put their hand to the plough in service in the Kingdom of God.

Doesn't the Rapture Happen Before Christ's Coming?

It has almost become the accepted view in many areas of Christendom that the church will be snatched away or raptured seven years before Christ appears and sets up His Kingdom. We call this the Pre-Tribulation Rapture theory or 'pre-trib' for short, as people holding this view believe the church will be raptured before or pre the Great Tribulation spoken of by Jesus in Matthew 24 verses 9 to 28. People who teach this relatively new doctrine say that we are not to look solely to Christ's second coming because He is actually coming two more times, once in secret for His church and then seven years later openly where everybody sees Him. This of course means that the church avoids the Great Tribulation that they say will occur during these last seven years; those of us who are raptured will be in heaven during this time of trouble on the earth and will return with Christ when He descends to the earth in full view of all to finally set up His Kingdom.

Of course if we read what the angels told the disciples as they watched Jesus ascend through the clouds into heaven that He would return in **exactly the same way** (Acts1:11) we would dismiss this teaching out of hand. Why would the angels say such a thing to people who would obviously have been raptured seven years previously assuming the return of Christ had happened in their lifetime? Why would the angels indicate that this is what we are to be looking for if we're actually going to be secretly raptured seven years **before** Jesus comes again in the clouds of heaven? Indeed Jesus Himself plainly stated that we were not to look for so-called mysterious or hidden comings (Matt.24:23-27) but to look for the **sign of the Son of Man** appearing in the sky, an event that will be seen by all.

> **"For just as the lightening comes from the east
> and flashes even to the west, so will the coming
> of the Son of Man be….But immediately AFTER
> the tribulation of those days the sun will be
> darkened, and the moon will not give its light,
> and the stars will fall from the sky, and the
> powers of the heavens will be shaken. And then**

> **the sign of the Son of Man will appear in the
> sky, and then all the tribes of the earth will
> mourn, and they will see the Son of Man coming
> on the clouds of the sky with power and great
> glory. And He will send forth His angels with a
> great trumpet and they will gather together His
> elect from the four winds, from one end of the
> sky to the other** (detailing the rapture or
> gathering of the church) ," Matt.24:27-31.

In my opinion a pre-trib rapture does not make sense because there is no secret rapture spoken of in scripture. The day of the Lord will certainly come as a, "Thief in the night," (I Thess.5:2), but this is speaking in relation to the fact that **this day** will steal up on people and they will not be prepared for it. It does not mean that Jesus will sneak into our world, secretly rapture His people away and nobody will realise what has happened for the next seven years apart from the fact that Christians are missing everywhere. No! In the very next verse of I Thessalonians chapter 5 the apostle Paul explains that while people are saying, "Peace and safety!" destruction comes upon them suddenly like labour pains upon a woman with child and they will not escape (I Thess.5:3). This does not sound anything like a secret rapture that people try and put forward today in support of the pre-trib rapture. The day itself will sneak up on them like a thief in the night, but what happens on that day will be very public indeed, just as Jesus and His apostles said it would be. Jesus will return exactly as He went into heaven as the angels said and exactly as Jesus Himself said He would in Matt.24:27-31, Mk.13:24-27 and in Lk. 21:27-28, that is **after** a period of great tribulation. This is when He raptures or snatches the church away, precisely as Jesus said He would in the gospel accounts just listed, an event that will be earth shatteringly public and visible to all!

Unfortunately due to its strong marketing and popularisation by various high profile authors in these days, some denominations have even put a pre-trib rapture as one of their articles of faith to which they subscribe. I too used to hold to this line of thinking (because I read it in my prophesy books) and would attempt to show people the chronology of end time events I had read in these books. The only problem was, every now and again as I read the Bible I would come across a verse that inferred this was not the case and even directly contradicted it! This troubled me very much; what I would normally do is go straight to my prophesy books and allow them to set my mind right on the subject. Then there came a day when the thought occurred to me, "Why don't I actually accept what the Bible seems to be saying, and take the risk that it may change what I'd previously believed?" This was a novel thought and one that has changed the whole direction of my life and ministry.

In a sense I am hesitant about even talking about this subject as there are people who hold to this doctrine so passionately that if they see someone does not agree with their cherished viewpoint they completely ignore anything else they have to say as well. I have unfortunately seen this happen; if the beliefs we hold are so shallow and tenuous they cannot be challenged I would suggest those beliefs are worth little. Perhaps some believe in a pre-trib rapture due to the overwhelming number of ministries, books, CDs and DVDs that actively promote this teaching in these days. Sometimes it is because they have a strong viewpoint on the place of the nation of Israel in the end times, and they **mistakenly** believe that a pre-tribulation position is the only one that will accommodate this view. I can say categorically that **it is not.** I felt ignoring this subject would not be helpful to those people who like me, used to be confused about this issue. Additionally whilst holding a pre-tribulation view on the surface of things may not seem to cause too much of a problem, the doctrines and expectations that are aroused by and that logically flow from such a view **become** a serious problem, even to the point of denying the centrality of the cross of Jesus Christ, a majorly serious issue indeed!

Many people will think, "Well what's the big deal anyway whether you believe pre, mid, post or even some other type of trib! When Jesus comes back we'll find out anyway so what does it matter?" I can completely understand why some people feel this way, especially after personally wrestling with the pre-trib viewpoint which in my experience hugely **over-complicates** the whole area flying in the face of the most obvious and plain rendering of the texts involved. It would be so much easier to just **allow the Bible to speak for itself** without having to look to others all the time to explain it to us. In a sense one could argue what does it matter whether someone believes in a pre-trib rapture? In some ways I'm sure there will be those people who **passively** hold to this view and it really doesn't make any difference to their faith walk with the Lord. For them it really doesn't matter whether they believe pre, mid or post trib! However the problem arises when we start seeing everything **through** the pre-trib viewpoint and we then start interpreting the Bible **according** to what this model tells us. This can have devastating consequences to how we read and apply the Bible to our ordinary lives. In this context, how we see the coming of Jesus matters a great deal because believing in a pre-tribulation rapture causes your understanding of scripture to be coloured into viewing everything through 'pre-trib glasses.' Everything you read has to fit into the pre-trib scenario or model and this causes verses to be taken out of context or even ignored as we surmise that, "Oh that doesn't apply to me because I won't be around during any tribulation," or, "These verses only apply to people unfortunate enough to find themselves in the Great Tribulation so I can just ignore them as I won't be there," or even, "The Kingdom parables don't apply to us because we'll be raptured up into heaven already." It also matters because the logical outworking of this theory results in heretical beliefs and also because it is a foundational truth of the faith (Heb.6:2 - the, "Resurrection of the dead") that **cannot** and **should not** be misrepresented.

I have the feeling that when Jesus said, "At that time many will fall away," (Matt.24:10) speaking as He was of a time at the end when His people are persecuted by all nations, this may well include many pre-trib believers. Having been told they will be, "On the first train out of there," (as I have heard the rapture being described by some modern preachers today) before any persecution arises, they are highly likely to be offended and caused to stumble as they still find themselves on terra firma when this tribulation takes place. I will try and tackle this whole issue in brief, as to properly address the subject would probably take another book! It is interesting (and quite scary) to note that the apostle Paul had harsh words to say about individuals who gave a different time frame to the resurrection than that clearly given in scripture, saying they had, "Gone astray from the truth," and that their teaching would, "Spread like gangrene," (II Tim.2:16-18). The resurrection from the dead (and by implication the rapture of God's people that happens at the same time as clearly stated in these scriptures: I Thess.4:15-17, Lk.21:25-28, I Cor.15:51-52 etc) is a **foundational teaching** of the Christian faith (Heb.6:1-2) and we mess with it at our peril.

Do you realise that not one scripture in the entire Bible directly says there will be a pre-tribulation rapture? It is all based on **indirect** scriptures and an assumption that God **cannot** deal with Israel whilst the church is still around. This did not seem to be too much of a problem for our Lord in the days of the early church when God's grace was poured out upon both Jew and gentile (Acts 2:5-41, Acts 10:44-48, Acts 11:19-21) but for some reason becomes a problem in the end times for some people. There is a truth that the gentiles must be taken out of the way before grace will once more be given to the Jews en-masse and I will talk about this later; however this is not the same as saying the church has to be raptured seven years **before** this grace will be poured out upon Israel.

Believing that God has to take the church out of the way before He can deal again with the Jews as He did under the Old Covenant, leads in effect to a **denial** of the completed work of Christ on the cross. This is because proponents say that the people of Israel have to go back to keeping the Law of Moses again during this seven year period as the 'church age is now finished'. They say because the age of grace is now finished, God reverts back to acting as He did in the Old Testament and the Jews will have to keep the Law of Moses again in order to be acceptable to God or even 'saved.' This inherent flaw in the pre-tribulation theory is often overlooked by people who believe in this theory

41

and skirted around by those who promote it. By putting forward this viewpoint they conveniently ignore verses such as Christ's sacrifice being, "Once for all," (Heb.7:27), that the former commandments were, "Weak and useless," and, "Made nothing perfect," (Heb.7:18-19), and those who try and keep the Law have been, "Severed from Christ…have fallen from grace," (Gal.5:4). The Bible says very clearly that the faith we hold, "Was **once for all** handed down to the saints," (not 'once for all until the rapture occurs,' Jude 3), and now that faith has come, "We are no longer under a tutor," (i.e. the Mosaic Law, Gal.3:25) and that, "As many as are of the works of the Law are under a curse," (Gal.3:10). This strict dispensational view of things flies in the face of the whole gospel message and would have been abhorrent to the apostles. For sure Israel will be brought in once again in the last days, but this **must** be through faith in their Messiah, **not** in the empty rituals and works of the Law that can save nobody. Does not the scripture say this plainly enough in Romans chapter 3 and verse 30, that God will justify the circumcised (the Jews) and the uncircumcised (the gentiles) through **faith**, not through the works of the Law. People who infer otherwise are badly mistaken!

Not one scripture clearly speaks of the 'pre-tribulation' rapture; however there are verses that **directly** contradict it. II Thess. 1:6-10 shows that there is coming **a day** in which the Lord will afflict those who persecute His people and give relief to those who suffer for the sake of the Kingdom of God, as it says in verses 6 to 10:

> **"For after all it is only just for God to repay with affliction those who afflict you, and to give relief to you who are afflicted and to us as well WHEN THE LORD JESUS WILL BE REVEALED FROM HEAVEN WITH HIS MIGHTY ANGELS IN FLAMING FIRE, dealing out retribution to those who do not know God and to those who do not obey the gospel of our Lord Jesus…when He comes to be glorified in His saints on that day, and to be marvelled at among all who have believed."**

The apostle Paul says that when the Lord Jesus is revealed in glory with His mighty angels in flaming fire (without doubt His second coming in the sky visible to all), He will punish His enemies and give relief to those like the apostle Paul and the church at Thessaloniki, who were undergoing persecution for their faith. Paul phrases the sentence as if this momentous event would include him and the believers at Thessalonica if they were still alive at that time. He says it would happen on **the day** (singular) when Jesus comes to be glorified in His saints and marvelled at among all true believers. Surely if Paul believed in a pre-tribulation rapture, he would have made it clear that the relief he is talking about here actually happened seven years **prior** to this event taking place. He did not, because he did not believe in a pre-tribulation rapture. He believed God would give them relief and punish His enemies on the **same day**, the day when the Lord Jesus was **revealed** from heaven and not before. It could not be clearer.

Similarly in II Thess.2:1-3 the apostle Paul says plainly that the coming of our Lord Jesus Christ and **our gathering together to Him** will not happen before the great falling away or apostasy occurs first (prophesied by Jesus in Matt.24:10-13) and the antichrist is revealed (again prophesied by Jesus in Matt.24:15). Our gathering together to Him is the rapture and resurrection, and these verses show that this will occur at the **coming** of our Lord Jesus Christ, and **after** the apostasy and the antichrist is revealed. This would put the rapture and resurrection as happening after the apostasy described in Matt.24:10-13, in fact **exactly as it is plainly laid out** in the chronology of events given by Jesus in Matthew chapter 24 and Mark chapter 13. Also as almost all commentators say the antichrist will be revealed at the beginning of the 3½ year period called the Great Tribulation, how can the rapture have occurred before this point? According to the scriptures it cannot.

Some people say, "God would never allow His church to go through the great tribulation. That's like making your bride go through the Vietnam War before marrying them!" I've actually heard preachers say this. Such people have no idea of church history and how many believers down the centuries have been persecuted even to death, starting from the early church right up to the present time in places like China, Saudi Arabia and Sudan. My own wife went through the communist persecution in Bulgaria and I can say true believers have always been and will always be persecuted. Jesus said it would happen (John 15:20 & 16:33) and history teaches us that this is so. Not that we particularly look for it or have a strange death wish; however it is coming and just because we don't currently experience it in our comfortable Western societies does not mean it is not going to arrive and does not alter the fact that many of our brothers and sisters around the world are experiencing it on a daily basis. The Lord Jesus, "Rescues us from the wrath to come," (I Thess.1:10), but there is a huge difference between experiencing demonically inspired persecution, the hatred of evil men, and the effects of God's judgement living as we do in a fallen world under God's curse, with the **wrath of God** that will be poured out upon sinful men at the time of the end. The scriptures say that the Lord will allow the antichrist to, "Make war with the saints and to overcome them," (Rev.13:7), "Overpowering them, **until** the Ancient of Days came and judgement was passed in favour of the saints of the Highest One, and the time arrived when the saints took possession of the Kingdom," (Dan.7:21-22). We all experience God's judgements to some extent because we live in an ungodly world that is under the curse of God. All true believers will know the wrath of Satan directed against them in some way; however this is nothing compared with the **furious wrath** of God that one day will be poured out full measure upon sinful man.

We could go on with so many other points such as the fact that Jesus repeats four times in John chapter 6 that the resurrection will take place on the, "**Last day**," (Jn.6:39,40,44,54), not seven years before the last day, a point then reiterated by Martha in John 11:24. Or we could mention that the apostle Paul tells us **exactly** when the rapture and resurrection will take place in I

Cor.15:52 namely, "At the **last trumpet**," (i.e. not before the first one as the pre-trib teachers would have us believe). This **last** trumpet is blown in Revelation 11:15 and its sounding prompts loud voices in heaven to say,

> **"The kingdom of the world has become the Kingdom of our Lord and of His Christ** (when? - at the sounding of the seventh and last trumpet of course!)**; and He will reign forever and ever....You have taken Your great power and HAVE BEGUN to reign. And the nations were enraged, and Your wrath came, and the time came for the dead to be judged and the time to reward Your bond-servants the prophets and the saints and those who fear Your name, the small and the great, and to destroy those who destroy the earth,"** Rev.11:15-18.

Surely it could not be any clearer could it? The rapture and resurrection happen at the sounding of the seventh trumpet, the time when Christ receives His rightful Kingdom; He judges the dead, rewards His servants and punishes the evildoers, all at His one and only coming. There are no two or even three comings as some suggest; there is only one.

In the previous chapter of Revelation, a mighty angel comes down from heaven and declares,

> **"In the days of the voice of the seventh angel, when he is about to sound, then the MYSTERY of God is finished, as He preached** (literally: 'preached the gospel') **to His servants the prophets,"** Rev.10:7.

What the angel is saying is that when the seventh angel sounds the last trumpet, the mystery of God as has been preached in the gospel given to us, will be **finished** or **completed**. What is this mystery? In Colossians chapter 1 and verse 27 the scripture says this:

45

> **"To whom God willed to make known what
> is the riches of the glory of this MYSTERY
> among the gentiles, which is Christ in you, the
> hope of glory."**

The mystery Paul is talking about is the amazing 'hope of glory' everyone who is joined to Christ has, the hope of the resurrection from the dead (or rapture if we are still alive) of putting off the body we live in or the corpse rotting in the ground, and being given an **immortal body** of power and glory that we will live in forever. Death will not be able to hold us, as it was unable to hold onto Christ who went before us. When the mighty angel announces the mystery of God will be finished at the seventh trumpet, he is indicating that our glorious hope of being **raptured** or **resurrected from the dead** will happen at the sounding of this last trumpet, exactly as the apostle Paul says it will in I Cor.15:52. We will leave our old mortal bodies behind with all their weaknesses and limitations and will be given a new body of power, clothed with glorious immortality. This happens at the **last trumpet**, when the Lord Jesus Christ is revealed from heaven for all to see. What a tremendous hope we have!

The apostle Paul also speaks of this mystery that gets finished at the seventh trumpet in Ephesians 5 verses 31 and 32:

> **"For this reason a man shall leave his father
> and mother and shall be joined to his wife,
> and the two shall become one flesh. This
> MYSTERY is great; but I am speaking with
> reference to Christ and the church."**

Paul likens the coming together of a husband and wife in sexual union on their marriage day as a picture of how the mystery of God is going to come about and be revealed. What is the Lord Jesus coming to do at His glorious appearing? He is coming to **take His bride** who has made herself spotless, holy and blameless (Eph.5:27), ready for Him. He is coming to **consummate** the marriage and make His bride fruitful; He is coming to be joined to her forever - the marriage of the Lamb has come, the joining of Christ with His bride the church. And when does this mystery get fulfilled or 'finished'? At the seventh and last trumpet when the kingdoms of this world become the Kingdoms of Christ, the dead are raised imperishable and those who are still alive are snatched away in a flash, in the twinkling of an eye, all happening on the **same day**. In no way can all these events happen on two days separated by an interval of seven years. The Bible clearly shows they happen **together on the same day.**

I have never met a person who came to believe in a pre-tribulation viewpoint from reading the Bible alone and I guarantee you have not either. Yet I have met many who came to believe it (including myself) from reading other people's books or listening to their preaching. What does this tell us? Quite simply that the Holy Spirit is **not leading** people to such a conclusion; we are getting it from men and their ideas, thoughts and opinions. This is the wrong way round!

For all the points raised above (and more not mentioned for the sake of brevity) I now do not believe in this pre-tribulation rapture. That is not to say that I cannot fellowship with or even learn things from people who hold this view. Nor does it mean I do not believe in the rapture. The snatching away or gathering of God's people will **certainly occur;** however as the early apostles believed it would happen **after** a period of tribulation and **concurrent** with the Lord's glorious appearing (I Cor.15:23, I Cor.15:51-52, I Thess.3:3-4, I Thess.4:15-17 [note the word 'we' used by Paul], I Thess.5:2-4, II Thess.1:4-10, Dan.7:21-22), and indeed Jesus Himself said the same thing in His Olivet discourse (Matt.24:9-31, Mk.13:9-27), I have also come to the same conclusion.

The Bema of Christ

The word commonly translated judgement seat or tribunal in the New Testament is the Greek word bema. Whilst not true for everyone especially those outside of Western - style Christianity, I believe it is fair to say that the doctrine of the bema must be one of the most misunderstood teachings in certain quarters of the church today. As far as I have seen it is **rarely mentioned**, and when it is, it is usually pictured as the place where all Christians receive their rewards before entering the heavenly Kingdom. This of course fits very nicely with our preoccupation in the West of assuring all who come to faith in Christ that they are eternally secure no matter what they do. Proponents of this view cite the ancient Olympic Games as their point of reference, as the athletes used to appear before the bema to receive their victory laurels. However, let me ask you this question. Are we supposed to interpret God's Holy Word according to the standards set by a pagan, ungodly event, or should we allow the Bible to explain itself, considering that how the word is used throughout the scriptures would give a good indication of how we should interpret it in this passage? I personally tend toward the latter viewpoint.

The word bema is used in four separate incidents recorded in the Gospels and in the Acts of the Apostles. The first references are in Matt.27:19 and Jn.19:13 where Jesus appears before the bema of Pilate. Now could it be said that Jesus was appearing before the bema of Pilate in order to be rewarded for being such a good Messiah and preacher of righteousness? Maybe Pilate really liked Him, had heard some of His messages and put Him before his judgement seat in order to really bless Him? Or is it not true that Jesus was on trial for His life and the evidence of His guilt or innocence would be heard before the bema leading to His conviction or acquittal based on what evidence was presented? The answer is obvious.

The second time it is mentioned is in Acts 12:21 where King Herod sat on the bema whilst the people of Tyre and Sidon sought his favour as they relied on him for their food supplies. Depending upon his reaction they would be well fed or go hungry. It could go either way.

The next time the bema is mentioned is in Acts 18:12 when the apostle Paul was brought before the bema of Gallio proconsul of

Achaia by the Jews intent on stopping his ministry dead in its tracks. Now again, could it be said that the Jews were so impressed at Paul's ability to turn people away from their empty rituals and traditions that they made sure they would organise with the ruler of the synagogue Sosthenes, to bring Paul before the bema of the proconsul in order to reward him really well? Did the Jews beat Sosthenes because they were so annoyed their chance to bless Paul publically had evaporated? Or is it not true that they brought him here because this was the place where sentence was pronounced depending on the evidence presented and they hoped to swing the evidence against him?

The final occasion is found in Acts 25:6 where the apostle Paul appears before the bema of the Roman governor Festus. Once again he is brought by the Jews intent on doing away with him, and once again the evidence for his guilt or innocence is presented to be examined and judgement passed.

In no way can we read the Bible and think the bema is the place where we all receive rewards for good behaviour and that is it. It is **patently obvious** that Biblically speaking the bema is the place where the facts are examined and judgement is given either way depending upon the **evidence presented**. This is why the apostle Paul says in II Cor.5:10 that each of us (church people) must appear before the bema to be recompensed for the deeds done in the body, according to what we have done, **whether good or bad.** He then goes on to say in verse 11, "Therefore knowing the fear of the Lord, we persuade men." The word translated fear here is more than just fright or awe; the New King James Bible translates it, "Terror." It literally means to be put into fear. No - one would fear if they were being brought before the bema to see how big their reward was. No - one would be in terror if they knew they were guaranteed a place in heaven, just their reward may not be quite as big as the man next door. There is fear and even terror because the genuineness of your faith is going to be assessed according to what you have done in the flesh and many who thought they had an alive faith will find out that it has been dead for many years.

The book of James makes it clear that faith without works is dead (Jam.2:26). If someone claims they have faith but have no deeds to back up their claim, they are deceived and on dangerous ground. An alive faith produces good deeds as surely as night follows day. There are no ifs or buts, if you truly have faith, you **will** have good deeds to show for it, end of story. Unfortunately today there are many people who live their 'Christian' lives thinking all is OK because the pastor said they were saved and therefore they must be fine. Churches are often full of individuals who can relate their 'salvation experience' but if their lives were examined they would have no **evidence** to show for the faith they say they possess. James says such people have a dead faith, and this is **not enough** to ensure the salvation of your soul. Only an alive faith will do that. An alive faith is the **only thing** that will be in your favour at the judgement seat of Christ, the only thing that stands between you and hell - fire damnation. If I were to ask you, if your eternal soul were before the judgement seat of Christ tonight, would there be enough **evidence** to convince the judge that you are in the faith or have you been deceiving yourself and everyone else around you?

Chapter 5
The Kingdom Parables

Many people have great difficulties in interpreting the Kingdom parables of Jesus because they seem to suggest that a division is going to happen at the coming of Jesus, a division between those who do their Master's will and those who do not. Now because so many new believers are told that as long as they've prayed the sinner's prayer and meant it with their whole heart, then they're saved, such parables present a **real problem.** Does this mean that even if you come to faith in Jesus Christ, you can still end up thrown into hell like the lazy, wicked slave of Matt.25:30 or the goats of Matt.25:46? It certainly does.

Understand the Parables, Understand the Kingdom

The parables Jesus gave us are **key** to understanding the gospel of the Kingdom. Parables of course are relatively simplistic stories that are put together and designed in such a way that by understanding them, we can then grasp deep spiritual truths we would otherwise struggle to comprehend. Unfortunately because the parables seem to suggest a great **separation** is going to occur at the return of the King's Son, a separation between **His own servants,** this flies in the face of much popular theology of our day. Therefore in practice, the parables are rarely mentioned, and if they are touched upon, it is usually in a very general manner. For example, we may hear a sermon about the importance of not burying our talents but using all the giftings the Lord has given us for His glory, a sermon that is based upon the Parable of the Talents recorded in Matthew 25 verses 14 to 30. Whilst the principle of using everything we have been given is an important point to make, this is **not** what the Parable of the Talents is all about. It is so much more than just this one point. Additionally we rarely go into the details of each parable and certainly never answer the glaringly obvious questions such as, "If I bury my talent does that mean I am in danger of being thrown into hell?" a question that probably everyone is thinking but nobody dares ask because of the ramifications it may have on our beliefs and lifestyle (I would also make the point that the word 'talent' in this parable does not mean gifting or ability, but is talking of an extremely valuable unit of money - the Master's 'possessions').

Too many people seem to dispense with the details Jesus gave in the parables, suggesting that because they are stories we should not attach too much prominence to them. Such people would never dream of doing such a thing to other statements made by Jesus but seem to feel very free to do so when it comes to the parables. In my opinion this is a **serious mistake** to make.

When Jesus interpreted His own parables He always took every point seriously and explained it to His disciples. He did not disregard anything. It is also clear to see that the items, objects or people mentioned by Jesus in His parables had particular characteristics that were supposed to point us to **spiritual characteristics and truths** we need to grasp. For example, in the parable of the Wheat and the Tares recorded in Matthew 13 verses 24 to 43, Jesus says that the wheat represents the sons of the Kingdom whereas the tares represent the sons of evil. To the Jewish audience listening, the connection between the two would have been obvious. In the natural, the wheat and tares looked almost identical; they often grew together and could easily be mistaken one for the other. However the wheat was good and nutritious whereas the tares were poisonous. They looked the same from the outside but inside they were completely different. Jesus said the devil sowed the tares **among** the wheat. In other words they are found in the same place as the wheat. They may both be sown in the 'field of this world,' (verse 38) but the enemy has planted his seed in order to confuse and mix with the true seed. Our Lord is not talking about people found in the church and those outside it. No, He is speaking of people who are found growing **together**; who look the same from the outside but in reality are completely different. This is clearly seen in verses 41 to 43 where Jesus explains what is going to happen at the time of harvest. He says,

> **"The Son of Man will send forth His angels,**
> **and they will gather OUT OF HIS KINGDOM**
> **all stumbling blocks, and those who commit**
> **lawlessness** (the tares), **and will throw them**
> **into the furnace of fire; in that place there will**
> **be weeping and gnashing of teeth. Then the**
> **righteous** (the wheat) **will shine forth as the**
> **sun in the Kingdom of their Father."**

The tares will be gathered from **out of the Master's Kingdom**, uprooted from being **alongside** the wheat, and will be thrown into the fires of hell.

Jesus takes something that was known in the natural to explain the way false and true believers sit alongside each other in churches, sing the same songs and join in the same activities. They look the same from the outside, it may be hard to tell them apart yet when the harvest time comes, a **division** takes place. The natural characteristics of wheat and tares combine to give us understanding of what Jesus is meaning, the lesson He wants us to learn. The details are **vitally important**.

Similarly in the parable of the sower which Jesus again explains to His disciples, the soil types reflect the various conditions found in the hearts of men. The way a plant grows in the soil is exactly the way the seed of God's word will grow in our hearts as we hear the, "Implanted word," (Jam.1:21). As soil is the perfect base from which a seed can hide itself, take root and grow, becoming in time a fruit - bearing plant, so our hearts are the perfect base in which the, "Imperishable seed," (I Pet.1:23) of God's Word can hide itself, take root and grow, becoming in time a fruit - bearing plant, the **new creation in Christ** grown up to maturity and useful in the Master's hands. The characteristics of the soil teach us spiritual truths about how our hearts operate and how the new creation can grow inside of us. This is why Jesus spoke about soil. He did not speak about water or snow covered fields; He spoke of soil because the **characteristics** of dirt and earth **perfectly reflect** the characteristics of the heart of man, and by understanding the natural lesson, we comprehend the more important **spiritual lessons** He was giving.

Similarly the characteristics of the thorns, how they can look so innocent and unthreatening yet in no time at all have grown around the plant and have crushed the life out of it, teach us what happens to our hearts when we allow worry, the deceitfulness of riches and the desire for other things to grow up in our hearts along with the new creation in Christ. The spiritual growth we have experienced may be real and powerful enough, but if we don't deal with the thorns, in no time at all they will have choked the plant making it unfruitful. At first these things may not look too threatening; we become blasé about the spiritual life that is inside of us and don't think the thorns can do us any harm; they look so small and insignificant. But we forget the warning given in I Cor.10:12 which says,

> **"Therefore let him who thinks he stands take heed that he does not fall."**

The thorns grow up very fast and in no time at all they have wrapped themselves around the plant and choked the life out of it. The new life in the plant was there for all to see; it had the potential to become tremendously fruitful. However the plant **never made it** because it **did not deal** with the thorns that were quietly growing up around it. An unfruitful plant will be cut down and thrown into the fire (Luke 13:6-9, John 15:1-6). This is a sobering lesson our Lord wants us to be aware of so we make sure the thorns do not grow up in our hearts! Jesus did not speak about dandelions, lilies or even rose bushes. He spoke about thorns because the specific characteristics of the thorns teach us specific lessons He wanted His disciples to know. The **details** contained in the parables are **extremely important.** Jesus never wasted His words, saying things He didn't think we needed to hear. Everything is important; every detail is a lesson He would have us learn.

Parable of the Dragnet

If we read the Kingdom parables of Jesus located in Matthew chapters 13, 22, 24, 25, and Luke 12 and 14, reading with an open mind and with no pre-conceived ideas, we will soon conclude that at the coming of Jesus a **separation** is going to occur, a division between wise slaves and evil slaves, bad fish and good fish, wise virgins and foolish ones, wheat and tares, faithful servant and lazy servant, prepared wedding guest and those who are not, sheep and goats. Let's take the parable of the dragnet found in Matthew 13:47-50 as a case in point:

> **"Again, the Kingdom of heaven is like a dragnet cast into the sea, and gathering fish of every kind; and when it was filled, they drew it up on the beach; and they sat down and gathered the good fish into containers, but the bad they threw away. So it will be at the end of the age; the angels will come forth and take out the wicked from among the righteous, and will throw them into the furnace of fire; in that place there will be weeping and gnashing of teeth."**

Jesus says the Kingdom is like a dragnet cast into the sea gathering fish of every kind. From the book of Revelation chapter 17 and verse 15 we understand that the sea or waters represent peoples, nations, multitudes and tongues. Jesus told His disciples that He would make them fishers of men, and over the years those that would heed the same call have sought to catch men in the net of the Kingdom of Heaven. Some are caught in the net, and some swim outside it. Those that come to the faith and begin the journey are like fish caught in the Master's net. Those outside the net have never come to the faith at all. They are still in the sea of the nations of this world. As long as the net stays in the sea, the fish swim around it relatively undisturbed.

However there comes a time when the net is dragged up onto the beach and the fish are taken out of the sea. Jesus says in Mark 13:27 that when the Son of Man comes, He will send out His angels to gather His elect from the four winds, from the farthest end of the earth to the farthest end of heaven. Jesus says the angels will take all the fish contained in the net and will sort the good fish from the bad. A **separation** will occur, not between those in the world and those in the church, but **between those in the net of the Kingdom of heaven.**

The angels, "Take out the wicked from among the righteous," and throw them into Gehenna, that is hell - fire. The bad fish look like the good fish, they swim alongside them and are even found in the same net, but they are not the same. They are bad fish and **unfit** for the Master. They are thrown away. The obvious question posed by this parable is, "Am I a good fish or a bad one? Just because I am swimming around with good fish, does that make me a good fish too?" By giving us this parable Jesus is warning us to settle these questions **before** He sends His angels to start the sorting process.

In the parable of the wise and evil slaves put over the Master's household (Matt.24:45-51), a parable clearly speaking of leadership in the church, the slaves are separated at their Master's coming, judged according to how they cared for those under their charge. If they fed their fellow slaves the proper food at the proper time (the proper food being the true gospel Jesus and His apostles taught and preached), they would be ready for the Master when He returned. The good slaves are blessed and put in charge of all their Master's possessions; the evil slaves who are found feeding only themselves and abusing the slaves under their control are cut to pieces and thrown in the place with the hypocrites where there is weeping and gnashing of teeth.

Parable of the Wedding Feast

Jesus said the Kingdom of heaven may be compared to a King who made a wedding feast for His Son. Straight away we can identify the King as God the Father and His Son as Jesus Christ. This seems relatively clear. He says that the Kingdom of heaven will be like a wedding feast given for the Son. Reading scriptures such as Eph.5:22-32, Rev.19:7-10 and Rev.21:2-4 we see that Jesus is the bridegroom, the church is His bride, and there is coming a day when the two will be joined together in holy matrimony. This day is called the marriage of the Lamb and clearly takes place at the Lord's second coming, the day He comes to receive His bride,

> **"In all her glory, having no spot or wrinkle or
> any such thing; but...holy and blameless,"**
> Eph.5:27.

The angel said to John in Revelation 19 verse 9,

> **"Blessed are those who are invited to the
> marriage supper of the Lamb."**

The King personally sends out His own slaves to those who have been invited to this marriage supper but incredibly finds that they are **unwilling to come!** He sends still more to give the good news of the royal banquet that is all ready for those **personally chosen.** The dinner is prepared, the oxen and fattened livestock kept only for the most special of occasions are all butchered and ready. It is a feast fit for a King, yet all the slaves hear are one excuse after another; the chosen ones pay no attention and instead get on with their own business. Others mistreat the King's slaves and even kill some of them. It is the height of rude behaviour and selfishness, the like that **cannot be tolerated** or ignored. The King is enraged and sends His armies to destroy those murderers and set their city on fire. From being the chosen ones, blessed to be invited to the marriage supper of the Lamb, they now feel the full force of the King's wrath as they are destroyed along with their city.

God made a covenant with Abraham and the children of Israel to be their God and they were to be His holy people. Due to their continual wickedness God sent them His slaves the prophets who time and again spoke to the people in the King's Name, reminding them of their heavenly calling. They were chosen to be a part of the King's wedding feast, to be joined to their God; to them belonged the adoption as sons, the glory and the covenants (Rom.9:4), but instead throughout their history they rejected the King and mistreated His servants the prophets. They despised the riches of His grace.

Despite all this during the ministry of Jesus, God's faithfulness to His people remained. Jesus had a mandate to preach only, "To the lost sheep of the house of Israel," (Matt.15:24) a task He stuck to throughout His short life, calling God's people to, "Strive to enter through the narrow door," (Lk.13:24) the door to the wedding feast in the Kingdom. However this still was not enough for the Jews of His day and they rejected His message killing Him in the process.

This was the final straw for the King; He sent His armies and destroyed those murderers, setting their city on fire. In AD70 the Roman armies under Titus finally managed to breach the defences of Jerusalem and put the city to the sword. Josephus the Jewish historian estimated that around 1,100,000 Jews were killed in this orgy of bloodshed and mayhem. The city itself was set on fire and would no longer be under the control of the Jewish people for the next 2,000 years. Jesus said that the King would send **His armies** to destroy those murderers. It is sobering to think that God considered the Roman armies as, "His armies," whom He sent to execute judgement upon His people.

> **"Behold then the kindness and severity of God; to those who fell, severity, but to you, God's kindness, if you continue in His kindness; otherwise you also will be cut off,"** Rom.11:22.

The King then sends His slaves to those who were not originally invited, to those found in the streets and highways. He says, "As many as you find there, invite to the wedding feast." The slaves go out and gathered together all they found, **both evil and good**, and the wedding hall was filled with dinner guests.

In Matthew 28 verses 19 and 20 Jesus gave us the great commission:

**"Go therefore and make disciples of all the
nations, baptising them in the name of the
Father and the Son and the Holy Spirit, teaching
them to observe all that I commanded you."**

Rather than just focus on the lost sheep of the house of Israel, we are now commanded to make disciples of **all the nations,** going to the streets and highways and inviting as many as we find there to the wedding feast. This is our commission we have received from the Lord. The King wants His house to be full. The slaves go out into the streets and gather together all they found **both evil and good,** and the wedding hall was filled with those reclining.

One day all those who have been invited to the wedding feast and have accepted the Master's invitation will be gathered together to the wedding hall, to be inspected by the King. This is a common theme in the Kingdom parables, the gathering together of those who have accepted the Master's invitation, of those who are **His servants** or a part of His household for the purpose of **inspection, accounting or judgement.** They are gathered in and the King comes to, "Look over the dinner guests," (verse 11). As He does so He comes across a man not dressed in wedding clothes.

All those invited to the wedding feast are highly privileged. Not everyone is invited; not everyone makes it into the wedding hall. However there is an **expectation** that if you are invited, it is incumbent upon you to **get ready.** Nobody just turns up to a wedding feast unprepared; even today in our relatively laid back Western culture, people would never think to arrive at a wedding without wearing the appropriate apparel. How much more when it is the greatest Royal wedding of all time, the marriage of the King's Son! To be unprepared for such a major event is unforgivable.

At the marriage of the Lamb, God's holy people are clothed in fine linen which stands for the righteous acts of the saints

(Rev.19:8). This is the correct dress for those invited to the wedding feast. Anything else is not classed as wedding clothes; it is **inappropriate dress**. Those invited to the marriage supper of the Lamb are expected to be preparing themselves by being rich in good deeds, clothing themselves in garments of salvation (Is.61:10). A true disciple of Jesus will always redeem the time given to them, being careful to engage in good deeds wherever possible. They will seek to know the voice of the Holy Spirit within and obey His holy promptings.

False disciples do not consider their ways but let opportunities for service slip them by. When Jesus said things like,

> **"Sell your possessions and give to charity;**
> **make yourselves money belts which do not**
> **wear out, an unfailing treasure in heaven,"**
> (Lk.12:33)

and,

> **"When you give a reception invite the poor,**
> **the crippled, the lame, the blind, and you will**
> **be blessed,"** (Lk.14:13 - 14),

they think, "Oh that's something for real extreme Christians, maybe if you're a missionary or in church ministry perhaps. Surely that doesn't mean me!" They fail to realise that God has not called them out of darkness in order for them to 'have a great life.' He's called them to **lose their lives** in this world in order to be ready for the Kingdom that's coming. He's called them to love their neighbour as themselves, to take the same devotion they have shown in loving themselves so chronically over the years and instead apply this devotion to others. This is **true discipleship** and obedience to this one commandment denotes whether you are a true son of the Father or not (Lk.6:35). Unfortunately in today's self - orientated church even this one command of Jesus has been twisted into an **excuse for loving self,** with people being told, "We must learn to love ourselves before we can truly obey this command of Jesus. If I can't first love myself, how will I ever be able to love my neighbour?" Again, God never told us to learn to love ourselves as we are **naturally expert** in such matters already! He told us to love our neighbour **in the same manner** and with the **same commitment** we have been showing ourselves over the years. Such a perversion and twisting of the gospel message is highly indicative of the true spiritual state of too many people in the West, 'spirituality' that has self embedded right at the heart.

False believers fail to appreciate the necessity of good works as the **evidence** of the faith they say they have within. A good tree will **always** produce good fruit whereas a bad tree will **only** produce bad fruit. A good tree **cannot** produce bad fruit; this would go against the grain of its very nature. It is an **impossibility**. If we are found to only have bad fruit at the judgement seat of Christ, can we still call ourselves a good tree, a true believer? It seems obvious that Jesus did not think so and nor should we. Disciples who are not dressed in wedding clothes are those who have become weary of doing good works and have reverted to their former selfish way of living. They did not heed the warning given in Galatians 6 verse 9:

> **"Let us not lose heart in doing good, for in due time we will reap if we do not grow weary."**

Selfish Christians are denying the very faith they say they hold. Putting self first is diametrically opposed to true discipleship, yet how many in today's church are **addicted** to a life of selfish fulfilment? Reading any list of the top selling Christian book titles today gives you all the answer you need. If it's not all about realizing **your** dreams and **your** vision and **your** desires and **your** success and enjoying **your** life what is it? Someone needs to wake up and realise the bride is being taught and trained on how to be **unprepared** for the wedding feast and it's not going to look pretty on judgement day. And first and foremost it's going to be the leaders, those who **allow and promote** this sort of rubbish to their sheep that are going to be dealt with first; those who rip off the sheep charging them money for what is in reality another gospel that will lead them straight to hell. As it says in Jeremiah 5 verses 30 and 31:

> **"An appalling and horrible thing has happened in the land: The prophets prophesy falsely, and the priests rule on their own authority; and My people love it so! But what will you do at the end of it?"**

When questioned by the King as to how he got into the hall with no wedding clothes, the unprepared guest is speechless. He has nothing to say and indeed there is nothing for him to say, no excuse that can be given for such a **profound error of judgement**. Many who think they'll 'get by' on the judgement day, who think they'll be able to explain all their great intentions to the King will have nothing to say on that day. They will be struck dumb and speechless.

The King commands His servants to bind this man hand and foot and throw him into the outer darkness where there is weeping and gnashing of teeth. It is a terrifying end to what once was the invitation of a lifetime. There is no other court, no higher authority to appeal to. This is the supreme court of all other courts and the decisions given are binding and final. He is lost for all eternity, his life destroyed as he **did not get himself ready** for the wedding feast. The invitation to the feast spelled out exactly how he should prepare and what clothes were necessary; it was plain enough in black and white. Was it that he just could not be bothered with the whole process of preparing for the feast, surmising that if he was so special as to be one of those called to the wedding feast surely they would let him in however he turned up? Or perhaps he heard that he was invited but didn't bother reading the invitation carefully enough to see that he was supposed to present himself at the hall in the correct attire - fine linen, bright and clean? Ripped jeans and a spotted t-shirt were never going to be acceptable. Or could it be that the King's servants told him he was invited to the marriage feast, but neglected to inform him of what the King expected of him. They invited him well enough, but did they ever explain to him how important it was to read the **whole** wedding invitation?

Our God has given us a **personal wedding invite** and an invitation to distribute to others. It is called His Word, the Bible and it contains everything we need to prepare us for the wedding feast. It tells us what the wedding feast will be like, who is invited, when it is going to occur and what we are expected to wear. It details exactly how we are to be preparing ourselves today to be ready for this greatest of Royal events. The question is, are we reading the wedding invitation and are we heeding its instructions. And if we are giving it out to others are we giving them the **whole** invitation or only the bit about them being invited? If we're not giving them the whole invitation or at least encouraging them to read it for themselves what good is it? Not everyone will want to hear the whole message of course and we cannot force feed people. However it's no good giving part of a message and allowing people to think that's all they need to know. That is how many will be left speechless at the judgement seat of Christ, because they never realised what was involved and they never counted the cost before starting to build (Lk.14:25-35).

Parable of the Wise and Foolish Virgins

When Jesus was on the Mount of Olives speaking to His disciples of the coming Kingdom, He gave them four parables to help them understand what He was referring to and what was actually going to take place. The second of these parables and one of the most striking of all is that of the Wise and Foolish Virgins (Matt.25:1-13).

In verse 1 Jesus says the Kingdom of Heaven is compared to ten virgins who take their lamps and go out to meet the bridegroom. The Kingdom of Heaven speaks of the church, not the world. People in this world who have never expressed faith in the Lord Jesus Christ are not a part of the Kingdom of Heaven; they will never take their lamps to meet the bridegroom because they don't believe in Him. As with most of the parables Jesus spoke to His disciples they are directed towards those who would consider themselves **His people**.

The parable speaks of a bridegroom who has delayed His coming. Who can this be other than the Lord Jesus Christ? It speaks of virgins carrying lamps. Lamps are the vehicles through which light shines to mark out our way in the darkness. In Psalm 119:105 it says this:

> **"Your word is a lamp to my feet and a light to my path."**

Similarly in Proverbs 6:23 it says this:

> **"For the commandment is a lamp and the teaching is light."**

The lamps represent the very Word of God itself, the **vehicle** through which **light** is supposed to shine to illuminate the way for us. Now if the lamps are representative of the Word of God, how many of the virgins possessed lamps? The answer of course is **all of them**, both the wise and the foolish. They all had the means by which they could be a light bearer and see their way through the darkness and into the wedding feast. Not one of the virgins could be excused on the basis that they never possessed a lamp; every one of them had the Word of God available to them. Additionally we can see that just possessing God's holy Word is not enough either. It has to be **filled with oil** for it to function correctly. The lamps Jesus refers to do not work unless they contain oil. Without a suitable fuel they may look great from the outside but will never serve a useful purpose except merely as a decoration. Their true function is **unrealised** unless they contain the oil which is necessary for a light to shine from them. So what is this oil being referred to in this parable?

Most commentators will agree that oil is a symbol of the Holy Spirit. But then so is running water, fire, wind and a dove. What **particular aspect** of the Holy Spirit's ministry is represented by the oil mentioned in this parable? In the Old Testament oil was used for a number of different purposes. It was used to fill the lamps and stand of the great candlestick found in the Holy Place in the temple. It was also used to anoint the chosen vessel of the Lord, much the way that Samuel anointed David as God's chosen king of Israel (I Sam.16:13). Prophets kept the anointing oil in a horn or flask which they carried around with them as they had need to use it. As we see that the wise virgins carried their oil in **flasks** along with their lamps (Matt.25:4), it seems to me that the Holy Spirit is showing us that the oil in this parable represents the particular **anointing** aspect of His ministry.

The wise virgins had oil in their flasks that allowed them to fully utilise their lamps in the darkness of the midnight hour in which the bridegroom returns. They had oil in their lamps, unlike the foolish virgins who did not prepare themselves correctly. A wise believer will be taking the time today to allow the Holy Spirit to **anoint their Bible reading**. One of the main reasons the Holy Spirit has been sent is to help us understand what the Bible is all about, as it says in John 14:26,

> **"But the Helper, the Holy Spirit, whom the Father will send in My name, He will teach you all things, and bring to your remembrance all that I said to you."**

So many people today speak of the anointing to heal the sick or the anointing to do miracles, but how often do we focus on the **most important** anointing of all, the anointing of God's Spirit upon His Word? For sure we need every anointing we can get; however the anointing of God's Spirit upon His Word is foundational for a successful Christian life and its importance **cannot** be underestimated. Indeed as this parable shows, unless we have this anointing upon our Bible reading, we will probably be unready for the bridegroom when He comes.

When oil is put into a lamp and is lit, light shines forth into the darkness. When the oil of the Holy Spirit is anointing our Bible reading, the scriptures come alive and a clear light shines out of them. What light do you think should be shining out of your lamp, out of your Bible when you read it? The Lord Jesus said,

> **"I am the Light of the world; he who follows Me will not walk in the darkness, but will have the Light of life,"** (John 8:12).

The whole Word of God is about a person called Jesus Christ, not the Jesus so many in the West have invented to fit with our consumer lifestyle, but the Jesus of the gospel accounts, the One who fulfils the pedigree set out for the Christ in the Old Testament. The whole Old Testament speaks about Him and in a mystery reveals the **new creation** that is in Him. He is the pre-existent Word that was spoken out on the first day of creation, the Light of life that had to shine before anything else could be created (Gen.1:3 & John1:1-5). He is our Passover Lamb (Ex.12:1-13 & I Cor.5:7), the Manna that fell in the wilderness (Ex.16:15 & John 6:51), the Rock that was struck (Num.17:6 & I Cor.10:4), the Branch that made the bitter waters sweet (Ex.15:25 & Jer.23:5), the Captain of the Lord's host (Josh.5:14), the Angel of the Lord who wrestled with Jacob (Gen.32:24-30), the scapegoat that bore the sins of the people in the wilderness (Lev.16:20-22 & Is.53:6), the bridegroom who comes to awaken His virgin bride in the middle of the night (Song of Songs 5:2).

What light do you have shining out of your lamp? Is it the Jesus who has been created over the years, the one who fulfils **our** expectations and desires, the man - made Jesus, or is it the One who is the fulfilment of the Old Testament scriptures? Is it the Jesus who says, "I've come to fulfil your dreams and visions!" or the One who says, "Whoever does not carry his own cross and come after Me cannot be My disciple," (Lk.14:27)? Is it the Jesus who says, "You need to find your best life now. Enjoy life - you have the victory!" or the One who says, "He who has found his life will lose it, and he who has lost his life for My sake will find it," (Matt.10:39)? Is it the Jesus who says, "If you knew your God - given authority in Christ you would never experience sufferings or trials," or the One who says, "He who falls on this stone (talking of Himself) will be broken to pieces; but on whomever it falls, it will scatter him like dust," (Matt.21:44)? Is it the Jesus who walks around in designer clothes, is a multi - millionaire and drives the latest chariot specially imported from Egypt to his crusades, or the Jesus who likely had only one or two sets of clothes (Lk.3:11, Matt.27:35), had no place to lay His head (Lk.9:58) and had to borrow a donkey because He did not own one Himself (Mk.11:1-6)? Is it the Jesus who says, "Unless you confess God's Word enough or give a break-through offering into my ministry you won't get your miracle," or the One who says, "Does He who provides you with the Spirit and works miracles among you, do it by the works of the Law (i.e. by our own human efforts), or by hearing with faith?" (Gal.3:5), and, "May your silver perish with you, because you thought you could **obtain the gift of God** with money!" (Acts 8:20)? I ask you again, what light do you have shining from your Bible? Is it a light that has been manufactured by men, or the very Light of life that is true and brings life wherever it goes and to whomsoever it touches? God's Word literally pulsates with the Light and Life of God Himself. If you are not seeing and perceiving this Light, not experiencing the living words of God's Word as you read it, could it be that you do not have any oil in your lamp?

Jesus said that when the Helper comes, whom He would send us from the Father, the Spirit of truth who proceeds from the Father,

> **"He will testify about Me,"** (John 15:26) and,

> **"He will glorify Me, for He will take of Mine and will disclose it to you,"** (John 16:14).

The Holy Spirit's **main** ministry is to point people to Jesus and this is **especially** true when it comes to interpreting the Word of God. If we are not getting a greater revelation of Jesus or coming more intimately acquainted with Him as we read His Word, we have to start asking ourselves the question, "Does my lamp contain oil or is it bone dry?" Is Bible study a joy to be looked forward to, or a chore because it feels like we're feeding on dry bread? The manna tasted of wafers of honey; when we feed on God's Word, literally feeding upon Him who is the Word of God, the Manna that came from heaven, it should leave a sweet taste in our spirit. If it does not can we truly say the Holy Spirit is anointing our Bible reading?

In the parable of the wise and foolish virgins, Jesus says that just prior to the bridegroom's return, **all** the virgins slumbered and slept (Matt.25:5). It was not just the foolish virgins who were asleep but the wise also.

Jesus spoke this parable during the time of Passover in Israel. We know that during this festival the rabbis would read from the Song of Songs in the synagogues. If we look into this book we find that a central part of it is describing and contrasting what happens to two virgin brides waiting for their beloved. One is spoken of in chapter 3 verses 1 to 4 and the other in chapter 5 verses 2 to 7. The striking thing is like the wise and foolish virgins, they are both in bed sleeping.

The first virgin bride described in chapter 3 gets herself out of bed and takes the time to seek the one she loves. She doesn't find him but instead of giving up she **continues** in her pursuit of him. Around the city, street and squares she goes, always on the look-out, searching for him with **all her heart**. Eventually after much searching she finds him, holds onto him and does not let him go. You could say she holds onto Him with an iron grip. They are joined together and have a wonderful future ahead of them of marital bliss; it is her best dream!

The same however cannot be said about the second virgin bride described in chapter 5. This virgin is also asleep in bed and her lover comes not during the daytime, but **in the night**. Remember Jesus said that the bridegroom would come at the midnight hour, the deepest and darkest point of the night. Night - time represents the ascent of evil and persecution against God's people (Lk.22:53, John.9:4, John 13:30). Jesus of course said that just prior to His return when He comes to take His virgin bride to Himself, there would be an increase in wickedness and indeed a wholesale persecution launched against His people (Matt.24:9-13). The problem for this virgin is that she is just too comfortable in bed. It says in verse 3 that she has taken off her dress or robe and doesn't want to bother putting it on again. As we saw in the previous parable, clothes represent garments of salvation and good deeds done by true believers. To be ready for the wedding feast we must be dressed in the **appropriate manner.** This virgin has taken off her dress and doesn't want to put it back on. That means she once had it on but has now taken it off. She has **given up** walking in the righteousness of Jesus and has become weary of doing good deeds. She no longer has any inclination to walk as Jesus and His apostles did.

It also says she has washed her feet and no longer wishes to dirty them by having to open the door. Spiritually speaking she has taken off her shoes and has no desire to put them back on as it would all take too much time and effort. She is no longer interested in inconveniencing herself for the sake of the gospel as she is far too comfortable in bed. In Ephesians chapter 6 the apostle Paul is exhorting the church at Ephesus to be **fully clothed** as a good soldier of Jesus Christ. He urges them to take up the full armour of God, which includes in verse 15, making sure their feet are shod with the preparation of the gospel of peace. Having shoes on in this context is akin to doing the work of an evangelist or preacher, either from behind a pulpit or more likely in our normal daily lives, sharing the good news of the gospel of peace through our words and lifestyle. As it says in Rom.10:14-15,

> **"How then will they call on Him in whom they**
> **have not believed? How will they believe in**
> **Him whom they have not heard? And how will**
> **they hear without a preacher? How will they**
> **preach unless they are sent? Just as it is**
> **written, 'How beautiful are the feet of those**
> **who bring good news of good things!'"**

This virgin bride through whatever circumstances in life has stopped sharing the good news of the gospel of peace. Both through her words and lifestyle she is no longer fulfilling the great commission (Matt.28:19-20), no longer being salt in the earth

(Matt.5:13). She has decided rather to hide her light under a bushel (Matt.5:15) and can no longer bring herself to dirty her feet in obedience to her Master. She is no longer about her Master's business. This virgin is lying in bed undressed, without the full armour of God, unprepared to inconvenience herself for her Lord, completely unready for the arrival of her bridegroom. The problem is, she seems **oblivious** to her predicament and of the **impending disaster** that is about to strike.

Eventually she drags herself out of her comfortable bed and goes to open the door to her beloved. The scripture says that her hands dripped with myrrh, even on the handle of the bolt of the door. Myrrh as a spice was used to anoint dead bodies in Jesus's day. This virgin bride has been anointed for death and she does not even know it.

As she opens the door she finds to her horror that her beloved has turned away and has gone. She searches for Him but does not find Him, calls out to Him but He does not answer. Her previous apathy is replaced by a sense of urgency to find her beloved but alas, He is no longer around; she was not ready at the due time and He has gone from her. She is left **alone** and **abandoned**. The watchmen of the city find her; they strike and wound her, and take away her covering. She is left naked, beaten, ashamed and alone. All that she thought she had has now been taken from her. There will be no joyful wedding party or happy family life; she has lost it all due to her own **inability to get ready** for the arrival of her bridegroom. It is her worst nightmare!

When the bridegroom comes for the wise and foolish virgins at the midnight hour, the prudent are ready and go with Him to the wedding feast and the door is shut. All the virgins slept prior to the shout going up announcing the arrival of the bridegroom. However it was only the wise virgins who had **prepared themselves** and were ready for His return. Spiritually speaking they had got out of bed and searched and searched and continued searching for Him until they found Him. Jesus said,

"Keep asking and it will be given to you; keep seeking, and you will find; keep knocking, and it will be opened to you,"
(Matt.7:7-literal translation).

These virgins had done exactly that; they had taken the time **before the bridegroom came** to get oil in their lamps. Through faith, patience and diligence they had allowed the Holy Spirit to anoint their Bibles and Light had shone forth out of them. We can only come to know someone when we see them as they really are. If we are a wise virgin we will be coming acquainted with the true Jesus, the One who was the suffering Servant but who will be the soon coming King. It's all about knowing Him and more importantly, **being known by Him**. This is the critical issue that will determine whether we are ready on that day or not. Those who come to know Him will become like Him - full of faith, full of righteousness and abounding in good deeds. They know their Saviour and Lord and are known by Him; and they got to this place by making sure there was **oil in their lamps**. In verse 12 of the parable Jesus says to the foolish virgins,

"Truly I say to you, I do not know you."

This is the litmus test for all virgins who would seek to be ready for the Master at His return. Do we **know** the true Jesus, or are we putting our faith into **another Jesus** that men have created, a Jesus that does not conflict with our idea of how we should live our lives? If we would be a true disciple of Jesus Christ we no longer have any rights to what we do in our own lives. He is either Lord of all, or not at all. This is a scary thought if we really think about it and many will not be able to walk it out in reality. But the fact remains only those who know the Lord will be known by Him, and only these folk will make it into the wedding feast God is preparing for those who love Him with all of their hearts.

What do you have filling your lamp and what light if any is shining out of it? Do you have oil in your lamp? As it says in Ephesians 5 and verses 14 to 18,

> "Awake sleeper, and arise from the dead, and
> Christ will shine on you. Therefore be careful
> how you walk, not as unwise men but as wise
> (virgins), **making the most of your time,**
> **because the days are evil. So then do not be**
> **foolish** (like the foolish virgins), **but understand**
> **what the will of the Lord is. And do not get**
> **drunk with wine, for that is dissipation, but be**
> **filled with the Spirit** (and have your lamp filled
> with His Spirit too)."

Are we filled with the Holy Spirit and is He the One directing our
Bible study? Whatever it costs you, get oil in your lamp. A
magnificent future awaits those who get ready for their Master.

What about the Other Two Olivet Parables?

Jesus spoke four Kingdom parables at the end of His Olivet
discourse, two of which we have touched upon, one in brief and
one in depth. However what about the other two, the parables of
the talents and the sheep and the goats? Neither time nor space
permits me in this book to fully address these two parables which
in my opinion are often misunderstood by many believers today.
Later on in the next chapter I will address one of the problems
people tend to have with placing where the parable of the sheep
and the goats fits in with the order of end - time events. This
question unfortunately often trips people up when the answer is
relatively straight - forward if one looks at things without the
distraction of preconceived ideas that are usually just other
people's opinions formulated to suit their particular viewpoint.
However let me just say that what we see happening in the
previous two parables takes place again in the parables of the
talents and that of the sheep and the goats. Servants have been
entrusted with the Master's possessions or care of His people and
there is an **accounting** upon how faithful they have been to this
trust at His return. At the Lord's coming the slaves who used the
talents given to them are welcomed into the joy of their Master
whereas the one who did not is thrown into the outer darkness

where there is weeping and gnashing of teeth. Similarly the sheep are blessed by their Father and inherit the Kingdom prepared for them from the foundation of the world. At the bema of Christ, His glorious throne, the throne of David, their deeds speak for the alive faith they possess. They fed hungry and thirsty people, welcomed strangers into their homes and clothed those who were naked. They visited the sick and those unfortunate enough to find themselves in prison (in context talking of those imprisoned for their faith in Jesus Christ). They are truly the sheep of His pasture because they act as Jesus would. They are a blessed people. The goats however may look like the sheep, they may have been found in the same flock, but they are not sheep; they do not act as sheep do, and are **thrown out** to be punished in eternal fire. All seems okay until they appear before the judgement seat of Christ, but at this critical juncture their **deeds are not found complete** in the sight of their God (Rev.3:2). They are cast out.

Jesus Meek and Mild?

Those who only view Jesus as someone who is meek and mild, who is desperate to have our love and who cannot live without us, will have quite a shock at His judgement seat. Not only will people we considered believers be found on His left, but severe punishments will be meted out to many whose deeds are found wanting at the bema. In the parable of the faithful and wicked steward the Master puts in charge of His servants found in Luke 12 verses 42 to 48, the faithful steward is blessed by the Master and put in charge of all His possessions. However the wicked steward is cut in pieces, presumably by a severe flogging (verses 47 and 48) and assigned a place with the unbelievers. The shame (and of course pain) he feels will be immeasurable. The parable goes on to say that those who did not know the Master's will and committed deeds worthy of a flogging will receive few lashes, but the ones who did know and still did the same things, will receive many lashes.

Jesus speaks of His enemies being executed before Him (Lk.19:27) and of binding unworthy servants hand and foot before throwing them into outer darkness where there is weeping and gnashing of teeth (Matt.22:13). Jude declares that the blackness of darkness is reserved forever for those who are found **in the church** but are not the Master's sheep (Jude 13). Indeed it is sobering to see how Jude links the second coming of Christ with the judgement He executes on such individuals who sit in the same pews and sing the same songs, but who are not a part of the new creation in Christ. He says,

> **"It was also ABOUT THESE MEN** (the ones he had been speaking about earlier who, 'Crept in unnoticed,' and perverted the true gospel of grace, who sat with everyone else at the church love feasts as if they were true believers but cared only for themselves) **that Enoch, in the seventh generation from Adam, prophesied, saying, 'Behold the Lord came with many thousands of His holy ones** (the second coming) **to execute judgement upon all, and to convict all the ungodly of all their ungodly deeds which they have done in an ungodly way, and of all the harsh things which ungodly sinners have spoken against Him.' These are grumblers, finding fault, following after their own lusts, they speak arrogantly, flattering people for the sake of gaining an advantage,"** Jude 14-16.

Somewhere along the way they denied or departed from the faith, and now face the wrath of the Lamb without having their sins covered by His blood; they face the, "Blackness of darkness .... forever," (verse 13). I remember a time of being in an unfamiliar place at night - time with all the lights off, groping my way forward to try and find a light switch. As I felt my way around I could not see my hand in front of my face, it was so very dark. I suddenly had a slight inkling of what it will be like for those thrown into this black darkness forever, never to see the light of the sun again. It was an awful thought. When God sent the plague of darkness over the land of Egypt in the time of Moses, nobody moved from their place for three days. God said it would be a darkness that could be felt. This will be a terrible judgement to bear.

James speaks with good reason that not many should become teachers in the body of Christ, as these will, "Incur a stricter judgement," (Jam.3:1). He also mentions in James 2 and verse 13 that, "Judgement will be **merciless** to one who has shown no mercy." We must ask ourselves the question, do we show mercy to our brothers and sisters in our local church and around the world, or do we close our hearts to them? When we see our brethren struggling in third world countries does it spur us to action or do we lose sight of things as we contemplate which size of flat screen TV will go best in our lounge, or where we should spend our third holiday of the year? Do we hold onto bitterness and grudges and treat those we consider below us with contempt? Whether we like it or not, the honest answer to these questions will have **eternal ramifications** for us.

When the Son of Man comes and gathers us all before His judgement seat, a separation is going to take place, between those who are truly His disciples and those who are not. It is apparent from the scripture that **many** who thought they were standing firm will find to their horror that they were not at all but it will be too late (I Cor.10:12). When we stand before the bema, there will be no second chances. The day of the recompense of our God has arrived and He, "Will render to each person according to his deeds," (Rom.2:6). As the scripture says, it appears many will be caught out and not ready for His return despite the numerous warnings given.

> **"Not everyone who says to Me, 'Lord, Lord,' will enter the Kingdom of Heaven, but He who does the will of My Father who is in heaven will enter. Many will say to Me on that day, 'Lord, Lord, did we not prophesy in Your name, and in Your name cast out demons, and in Your name perform many miracles?' And**

then I will declare to them, 'I never knew you; depart from Me, you who practice lawlessness,'" Matt.7:21-23.

Chapter 6
The Immortals

Once this immense separation takes place, the righteous enter the Kingdom, inheriting the promises given through the prophets all those years ago. At the great gathering that has occurred, those who are worthy will have been changed in a flash, in the twinkling of an eye, their mortal bodies being replaced with immortal spirit bodies, empowered to rule and reign with Christ for all eternity. No longer will they be subject to decay or corruption, the aches and pains of this brief life. Our new bodies will not be weak and frail, but they will be bodies of power, as that which is mortal is swallowed up by immortality and death is banished in us forever! We will finally look like Him for we will see Him as He is in full resurrection glory. The true sons of God are revealed.

> **"For I consider that the sufferings of this present time are not worthy to be compared with the glory that is to be revealed to us. For the anxious longing of the creation waits eagerly for the revealing of the sons of God,"** Rom.8:18-19.

To those who are found in Christ at His coming, who have kept the faith till the end, fire will be used to test the quality of their works at the bema of Christ. As it says in I Cor.3:10-15:

> **"According to the grace of God which was given to me, like a wise master builder I laid a foundation, and another is building on it. But each man must be careful how he builds on it.**

> For no man can lay a foundation other than the
> one which is laid, which is Jesus Christ. Now
> if any man builds on the foundation with gold,
> silver, precious stones, wood, hay, straw, each
> man's work will become evident; for the day
> will show it because it is to be revealed with
> fire, and the fire itself will test the quality of
> each man's work. If any man's work which he
> has built on it remains, he will receive a
> reward. If any man's work is burned up, he
> will suffer loss; but he himself will be saved,
> yet so as through fire."

Many people confuse this passage with the judgement of all believers at the bema of Christ, surmising that if you don't get much of a reward because you have led a selfish 'Christian' life, at least you'll squeeze through the door, "Saved yet as through fire." Many comfort themselves with these words thinking that it doesn't really matter how they live because at the very least they'll scrape through in the end. However those found with no evidence of an alive faith at His coming have **not** been building on the foundation which is Jesus Christ. They do not fit into the category of people to whom these verses refer. They do not qualify as these verses talk of those who have **built on the foundation which is Jesus Christ**, of those who have **kept hold of their faith,** not those who have **denied the faith** they once professed, who have been building their house on the sands of the ways and philosophies of this world rather than upon the foundation which is the Rock Christ Jesus (Matt.7:24-27). These type of people will be barred from entering the Kingdom.

Those who no longer have the foundation of Jesus Christ as the cornerstone of their lives will not have their good deeds judged as they are still in their sins. Any good deed they do will now be irrelevant in the context of gaining a reward from the Lord as sinful men cannot inherit the Kingdom of God (I Cor.6:9). If we have ceased building the house of our life on the sands of the ways and philosophies of this world to start building on the Rock

Christ Jesus only to turn around later and start building on sand again, we will one day see our house destroyed. There will be no reward for us. The scripture clearly says, "If I rebuild what I have once destroyed, I **prove myself** a transgressor," (Gal.2:18). These verses in I Corinthians chapter 3 talking about the testing of our deeds by fire are not referring to those who have once been in the faith but departed from it; they refer to those who will be found on His right at His coming, those who make it into the wedding feast, who are gathered up into the Lord's barn (Lk.3:17) at His coming. These are the ones who will be rewarded for the good deeds done in the body dependant on whether their righteous acts can stand the test of fire God is going to give them.

At the judgement seat of Christ our deeds will be measured and tested and rewards will be given according to the **quality** of our works. To those who have laboured in the faith, who have fed widows and orphans, have helped those who could not repay them, these will be repaid at the resurrection of the righteous. To some who have been found faithful in the things of this world, they will be given charge of cities; some will be given thrones for judgement. The 12 apostles of the Lamb will be given thrones to judge the 12 tribes of Israel (Matt.19:28) their names inscribed on the foundation stones of the wall surrounding the heavenly Jerusalem (Rev.21:14). Daniel 12 verse 3 states that those who have insight will shine brightly like the brightness of the expanse of heaven, and those who lead many to righteousness will shine like the stars forever and ever. The scripture also says that, "Star differs from star in glory," (I Cor.15:41). Though all those who inherit the Kingdom will have immortal resurrection bodies, some will be more glorious than others. Those who have learnt to become the servant of all will become ruler of all. Truly the last will be first and the first will be last (Matt.20:16).

Will only Christians Live in this Kingdom?

It is commonly supposed (mistakenly in my opinion) that only Christians will inhabit the Messianic Kingdom. A number of people draw this conclusion solely through holding or by being influenced by a 'pre-tribulation strict dispensationalist' viewpoint that gives a **very particular** interpretation of the parable of the sheep and the goats as recorded in Matthew 25 verses 31 to 46. They say that once the church is secretly raptured into heaven, there will be seven years of tribulation the world will go through, culminating in the glorious return of Jesus Christ to the earth with His saints. During these seven years 144,000 Jews get 'saved' and how the gentiles treat these 144,000 Jews is how God will judge the nations at His return as shown in the parable of the sheep and the goats (when, "All nations," are gathered before His glorious throne - Matt.25:32). They say that though all the parables preceding this one are referring directly to Christ's disciples (parable of the wise and evil slaves put over the Master's household, the wise and foolish virgins and the talents), this one is **only applicable** to a certain type of person, namely those gentiles who are left **after** the church has been raptured and are therefore still alive during the time of the Great Tribulation. In other words, they say the parable of the sheep and goats has **no relevance** to the church and so it is often passed over in preaching and teaching. This may seem like a relatively minor point as it is 'only one parable,' or even a mere technicality. However holding to this opinion **directly** leads to incorrect and inaccurate points of view regarding the Kingdom Christ is coming to establish. This is a much more serious situation and demonstrates how careful we must be to test everything we hear by the witness of the Spirit within and by the **whole** of God's Word, not just a few verses usually quoted incorrectly or out of context. Indeed I have seen whole doctrines created and justified by the erroneous interpretation of the parable of the sheep and goats.

Forgive me if I am sounding rather complicated for a moment, but to address this issue properly, by necessity I must go into some doctrinal detail. I will try to be brief. It is an unfortunate reality that once you start creating doctrines to suit a particular viewpoint (such as the pre-trib rapture or strict dispensationalism) the scriptures suddenly become very complicated and it feels like you need a PhD in Theology to understand it all! I believe the scriptures are very clear and fit together beautifully when we allow the Holy Spirit to guide our study, but get very complex and heavy to deal with once we start formulating our own doctrines and start trying to get the scripture to fit with them. If this gets all a bit complex for you, just skip down a couple of pages or so to the quotation from Ephesians 2:19.

There are a growing number of individuals, especially in 'prophecy/end times' ministries that actively promote the theory called 'dispensationalism.' What this theory means in a nutshell is that God deals with different peoples at different time periods in different ways. For example they say there are seven dispensations (or administrations of time) in which God deals with people in each dispensation in a different way. There has been the age of conscience, the age of human government, the age of the patriarchs and the age of law. They say that we are currently in the 'Age of Grace,' the time period dominated by the grace of God expressed through Jesus Christ, that followed the 'Age of Law,' (when God dealt with people through the Law of Moses). It is clear that we now live in the 'Church Age,' when God's grace has been poured out upon the gentiles and not upon the Jew (Rom.11:7-31), in stark contrast to the time **before** the Great Commission when God's dealings were almost exclusively directed towards the Jewish race. There is a **general truth** in these matters.

However many dispensationalists take this one step further by adding that God will **only** deal with the people of this world through the dispensational system He has put into place in each administration of time. They say God '**cannot**' deal with the Jews at the same time He is dealing with the gentiles in the church age, this despite the fact that He managed it quite happily for the first 100 years or so of the 'gentile church', a time when the church was indeed **dominated** by Jewish believers. By saying God 'cannot' do something, adherents of this viewpoint create a god who is not sovereign and is limited by things he has created. This is not the God of the Bible who alone is Sovereign, the God whom heaven and earth cannot contain (II Chron.6:18, Ps.113:5-6). The true God whom we serve is the great 'I Am,' not the great 'I Am

81

apart from what strict dispensationalism restricts Me to.' By limiting God to their particular system of theology they twist what would otherwise be a general truth and introduce serious error into the body of Christ.

Proponents of this form of Dispensationalism say that before God can deal with the Jews again He must take the gentiles out of the way. Again, in a sense there is a truth in this as the gentiles must, "Come in," (be gathered in as indicated by Jesus in Matt.24:31) before grace can once more be given to the Jews (Rom.11:25). However they then say this means God **has** to remove the church via a 'secret rapture' seven years **prior** to His second coming. The Bible does not say this but in order to fit the scripture around their system of theology (i.e. strict dispensationalism), they manufacture a whole doctrine of how God will finish the church age by rapturing the church into heaven so He is then able to deal with the Jewish nation once more, as if He couldn't deal with them with the church still around. I believe this doctrine which has been invented in the last 100 years or so appeals very strongly to certain men's desire to feel that they can compartmentalise the Bible into a logical order. There is logic in God's Word but it is not **based** on logic. It is based on the knowledge and wisdom of God Himself.

They say once the church has been raptured and is out of the way, God again deals with the Jews as He did in Old Testament times, with people offering temple sacrifices and obeying the Law of Moses again in order to be acceptable to Him. Imagine telling the apostle Paul that one day in the future the Jewish people will have to obey the Law again in order to approach God due to the rules laid down in the theological system of dispensationalism. I have a feeling this would have brought him into, "No small dissension and dispute," (Acts 15:2 NKJV) with the proponents of this point of view, much the same way he vigorously refuted this Judaization of the gospel in the days of the early church.

The strict dispensationalists say that during these final seven years of mankind's history, 144,000 Jews will miraculously be 'saved' (presumably by being observant Jews keeping the Law of Moses as the 'Age of Grace' is now at an end?), and they will evangelise the world through extreme persecution and adversity. It is difficult to know how they will 'evangelise' anyone if the Age of Grace is at an end and God is now dealing with people according to how well they keep the Mosaic Law. Be that as it may, the strict dispensationalists say that the parable of the sheep and the goats is how God is going to judge the gentiles or nations of the world (not the church) at His coming **after** the seven years in which He has been solely dealing with the Jews. Interesting that they only use this parable and conveniently ignore the other ones that certainly do not fit into their neat pre-tribulation dispensational view of the end-times.

They say that because the goats are separated from the sheep because of what they did or did not do, ("I was hungry and you gave Me something to eat…" Matt.25:35) i.e. because of their **works**, this **cannot** be the judgement of the church because we are saved by faith and not by works (Eph.2:8-9). They say that this parable must therefore be directed towards another group of people, namely the gentiles or nations who are around once the church has been taken out of the way. They conclude the parable of the sheep and the goats is the way Jesus is going to judge these nations depending on how they treated these 144,000 Jews spoken of in Revelation chapter 7 and verses 4 to 8 who come to 'faith' (faith in and through what I wonder?) and are sealed during this time of tribulation. People who hold to this view say that without exception, **all** the nations of the world (the Russians, Chinese, Americans, Bulgarians, Germans, English, Australians, Nigerians etc…) are separated at the coming of Jesus, so only those who have fed these hungry Jews, have given them drink and welcomed these Jewish strangers into their homes will enter the Messianic Kingdom at this time. All the rest will be cast from the Lord's presence into the everlasting fire prepared for the devil and his angels (Matt.25:46).

I suppose this would mean that it did not matter how good they had been in looking after their fellow gentiles, even those gentiles who were actively looking after the persecuted Jews (much like Corrie Ten Boom did by sheltering Jews from the Nazis in World War 2); they would still be thrown into hell because they expressly did not minister to this **specific** group of Jews. Pity the gentiles who never manage to meet one of these 144,000 Jews during these 7 years and are unable to minister to them. Presumably if we follow the logic of the strict dispensational argument, these gentiles will be thrown away to hell fire even though they were never able to make a choice based upon the criteria of judgement they receive in the separation of the sheep and the goats? How can Jesus say to them, "I was hungry and you gave Me nothing to eat," if they never even met one of these 144,000 Jews and had the choice to feed them or not? Of course it does not make any sense because it is not an **accurate** reading of the scriptures; it is a doctrine created by man for man.

All in all I feel this particular strict dispensational viewpoint of this parable is out of keeping with the flow and context of Jesus's words on the Mount of Olives, who He was directing this parable to (the 12 disciples as the founding members of the church), does not fit with the gospel which says that **each individual in the church** will be judged, "According to his deeds," i.e. by our good works or lack of them (Rom.2:6) and, "Faith without deeds is dead," (Jam.2:26), and does not properly deal with the dynamics of Romans chapter 11 and the return of Israel to their Messiah. It also simply does not fit with many other scriptures in the Bible (Is.60:3-16, Is.66:18-21, Zech.14:16-19, Rev.2:26-27 to name a few) which speak of nations, foreigners and strangers serving those who inherit the Kingdom, of people who are still around in the Messianic Kingdom but have never heard about the God of glory, of nations being punished for not obeying the Messiah and Him ruling over them with a 'rod of iron' i.e. exerting strict control over them. If the only gentiles in the Messianic Kingdom at this time are those who were gentile believers taken in the rapture or the gentiles who 'get saved' by treating the 144,000 Jews well during the great tribulation, who are these people who are supposed to be serving us in the Kingdom? Are we seriously trying to say that these nations, foreigners and strangers found in the Kingdom are gentile Christians who will serve the Jewish Christians, bearing in mind the apostle Paul's words in Ephesians 2:19,

> **"So then you** (gentile believers) **are no longer strangers and aliens, but you are fellow citizens with the saints, and are of God's household,"?**

I suppose some will say, "They are the children of those gentiles who 'got saved' during the Great Tribulation." The only problem with that (quite apart from the fact that the Bible never says this) is assuming some of these gentiles had children immediately and we waited for them to grow to a certain age before putting them to work (10-20 years?) who will be presenting offerings to Christ, who will be restoring the ruins and shepherding our flocks in the meantime? As we will see, the scripture is very clear that once Christ sets up His Kingdom the nations of the world will stream to Him, bowing before Him (and us as His ministers) and will bring the finest of gifts they can put together. Are we trying to say that Christ will sit on His throne but will have to wait for 20 years or so before the first batch of children had made it to a good enough age to do all the things listed in Isaiah 60 for example? Will we have to wait for some of them to be elected as kings so that the scripture can be fulfilled which says, "Their kings will minister to you,"? Maybe we will need to wait longer than 20 years; how about 30 or 40 years? The more you develop this line of thinking the more ridiculous it becomes. Taking the scriptures at face value we must conclude that there will be peoples and nations who are somehow spared at the coming of Jesus and who will enter the Messianic Kingdom as mortal people, even those who have never heard of Jesus before. This is not to say that they will inherit the Kingdom. Not at all. They will populate it and serve the immortals who are found to be worthy to take possession of it.

Though the parable of the sheep and the goats does speak specifically of the 'nations' or 'gentiles' (Greek word 'ethnos'), being gathered before His throne, Jesus **never** indicates in any way that it only applies to gentiles alive during the time of the Great Tribulation. He speaks the parable to **His disciples** that they **personally** should take note, and talks of the **evidence** He is looking for in a **true disciple**, the characteristics someone with an **alive faith** will be able to demonstrate at His coming. Jesus shows us what He expects His sheep to be like, not just in empty talk but in action and deed, ministering to their brethren and in that way, ministering to Him. It shows us how important it is to love our fellow brothers and sisters in the Lord, a theme **constantly reiterated** throughout the scriptures.

Rather than narrow interpretations down to suit a particular viewpoint I believe this parable is very much referring to those gentiles who would consider themselves believers in the Lord Jesus Christ both historically, now and in the future (Jesus constantly refers to the service they are supposed to be giving to their **fellow** believers, something an unbeliever would not even countenance). That means if you are a gentile Christian today, the parable of the sheep and the goats refers and **is applicable to you**! Of course this is the obvious conclusion anyone would come to if they read the words of Jesus and didn't pay so much attention to everyone else's opinions but who is brave enough to do that? Let's get back to God's Word and stop seeing things through everyone else's perspective.

The scripture is very clear that in the age in which we live, the Jewish people have experienced a hardening in part whilst grace has been poured out instead on the predominantly gentile church for a time and a season. The scripture says that this partial hardening will continue, "**Until the fullness of the gentiles has come in,**" Rom.11:25. What is the parable of the sheep and the goats talking about if it is not this 'coming in,' a gathering in that occurs **at** His coming and **not** seven years before it? The gentile church must be brought in before God's grace can once again be poured out upon the Jew. In the book of Genesis Joseph only revealed himself to his natural brothers at their second meeting, and only **after** the gentiles had first been taken out of the way (Gen.45:1). Jesus's own Jewish nation did not recognise Him at His first coming, but they will certainly do so at His second, as He comes in the clouds of heaven and gathers together the predominantly gentile church thus putting an end to the age of man.

Those from every nation, tribe, people and tongue will be brought before Him. All those who have begun the journey of faith will be brought before Christ's bema seat and will be judged according to their deeds, on how they treated their fellow brethren **exactly** as it is foretold in this parable. Some will have a genuine faith and some will not. The goats may have looked like sheep on the outside but what is on the inside, what makes them tick is now made evident. They may have been found in all the right 'spiritual' places, they may even have church titles and positions; but when it came to true compassion for their fellow believer, they were found wanting and will be cast away to the fires of hell.

The scripture is clear that there will be ordinary individuals living at the time of Christ's reign on the earth, even those who have never heard of Jesus Christ.

> **"For I know their works and their thoughts;**
> **the time is coming to gather all nations and**
> **tongues** (recorded in the parable of the sheep
> and the goats, the gathering of 'all nations'
> before His throne when Jesus returns). **And they**
> **shall come and see My glory. And I will set a**
> **sign among them** (the sign of the Son of Man
> receiving the Kingdom and seated on the
> glorious throne of David, dividing the sheep
> from the goats) **and will send survivors from**
> **them** (those who are found on His right at the
> bema of Christ, the immortals who inherit the
> Kingdom) **to the nations......that have neither**
> **heard My fame nor seen My glory. And they**
> (the immortals, God's sheep and now co-rulers
> of the Kingdom) **will declare My glory among**
> **the nations,"** Is.66:18-19.

If only Christians are living during this time, who will they be ruling and reigning over if there are no other people around? It does not make sense. In the book of Isaiah it speaks of foreigners building up our walls, their Kings ministering to us (Is.60:10); it speaks of strangers shepherding our flocks and foreigners farming our ground and tending our vines (Is.61:5). We will suck the milk from those around us (Is.60:16) and the wealth and glory of the nations will be brought to us along with the abundance of the seas (Is.60:5). Those who have oppressed and despised us will bow themselves at the soles of our feet (Is.60:14) and we will rule them with a rod of iron (Rev.2:26-27) in the authority of Jesus who is now the supreme ruler of the kingdoms of this world (Rev.11:15). The nomads of the desert will prostrate before Him, His enemies will lick the dust and the kings of the earth will bow down before Him and serve Him, bringing Him gifts, presents and the gold of Sheba (Ps.72:9-15). Those who choose to rebel against Him will receive swift judgement (Mal.3:5) and those who are left of the nations that went up against Jerusalem who do not obey His order to worship Him and celebrate the feast of Tabernacles will have no rain on their land (Zech.14:16-19). It even says we will pulverise many wicked peoples that we may devote their unjust gain to the Lord (Mic.4:13).

As Solomon established a Kingdom of wealth, power, wisdom and majesty, so Christ will do the same only on a much grander scale. Those immortals who share His rule will exert His authority wherever they go. They will be known as priests of the Lord, ministers of our God (Is.61:6), the holy people, the redeemed of the Lord (Is.62:12). It will be the greatest Kingdom ever known, dwarfing all others for splendour, reach, economy and efficiency. As those who administer it have already been proved faithful, no corruption will exist but righteousness will be the standard and justice the benchmark. The immortals will govern the nations and put down any rebellion against the rule of Christ. No rich man will be able to turn justice around with his money; no evildoer will be able to play the system, for those in control will not allow it. Wickedness will be judged swiftly and appropriately. People will rejoice for the immortals will govern in spirit and in truth with a righteous judgement.

What Will People Do?

The Bible does not go into great detail about what people will be doing during the millennial reign of Christ. However here and there we can deduce that those inhabiting the nations of the world at this time will be working as we do, and life for them will probably be organised in a relatively similar way to now, apart from the fact that allowance will no longer have to be made for systemic wickedness and corruption as it must be today.

It appears there will be people who build, shepherd, farm the land and fish the waters (Is.61:4-5, Ez.47:10). People will still need to eat and certainly we will not be floating about on fluffy clouds playing little harps singing lullabies! Industry will need to be attended to and life will have to be lived. Staple crops will need to be grown and various commodities will still be in demand (Ez.47:11). Fruit and nuts will become an important source of nutrition (Ez.47:12). People will still traverse the seas (Is.60:9), and gold and frankincense will still retain their value (Is.60:6). The earth's climate will still on occasion be terribly hot and there will be storms and rain every once in awhile, that is apart from on Mount Zion itself (Is.4:5-6). The worship of the One true God will become a standard glorious routine for the peoples of the earth (Is.66:23); and this will not be an empty ritualistic worship based on the Mosaic Law with all its regulations and traditions, but what these things point to **in Christ**, a worship given in Spirit and in truth (Jer.3:16-17, John 4:23, Heb.9:9-10).

Mount Zion, Centre of the World

The centre of this Kingdom will be located in geographical Israel; however it will not look like the Israel of today. The book of Zechariah chapter 14:10 says this:

> **"All the land will be changed into a plain from**
> **Geba to Rimmon south of Jerusalem; but**
> **Jerusalem will rise and remain on its site from**
> **Benjamin's Gate as far as the place of the First**
> **Gate to the Corner Gate, and from the Tower**
> **of Hananel to the King's wine presses."**

Somehow or other the land will be flattened out but Jerusalem itself will rise up as Mount Zion is raised to become chief of the mountains. All this will add to the **grandeur** of Mount Zion, the place where the Christ resides and Jerusalem His capital city, as this will be the dominant feature for miles around.

> **"And it will come about in the last days that the mountain of the house of the Lord will be established as the chief of the mountains. It will be raised above the hills, and the peoples will stream to it. Many nations will come and say, 'Come and let us go up to the mountain of the Lord and to the house of the God of Jacob, that He may teach us about His ways and that we may walk in His paths.' For from Zion will go forth the law, even the word of the Lord from Jerusalem. And He will judge between many peoples and render decisions for mighty, distant nations. Then they will hammer their swords into ploughshares and their spears into pruning hooks; nation will not lift up sword against nation, and never again will they train for war..... 'In that day,' declares the Lord, 'I will assemble the lame and gather the outcasts, even those whom I have afflicted. I will make the lame a remnant and the outcasts a strong nation, and the Lord will reign over them in Mount Zion from now on and forever. As for you, tower of the flock, hill of the daughter of Zion, to you it will come - even the former dominion will come, the Kingdom of the daughter of Jerusalem,'"** Micah 4:1-8.

Understanding I Cor.15:20-28 and how it leads to Revelation 22:3 shows us that the whole curse will only be lifted **after** Christ has reigned for a thousand years and He has delivered up the Kingdom to God the Father having put all enemies under His feet. However, **during** the millennial reign of Christ, physically speaking the earth will be much like it is today. The curse spoken by God in the Garden of Eden will only be lifted from Mount Zion and it will be a place that is obviously blessed by the Lord. Having said that I have no doubt the earth itself will **benefit greatly** from the lack of evil being practiced upon it during the millennial reign of Christ. Sin pollutes the land (Is.24:5,6,20) and conversely righteousness brings about God's blessing (Prov.11:19, 12:28, 14:34). These concepts may sound absurd to earthly minded people but spiritually speaking there will definitely be a knock-on benefit to the world for the righteousness being practiced upon it. It says in Psalm 72 and verse 16 that there will be an abundance of grain in the earth, even on the usually barren mountains tops, and its fruit will wave like the cedars of Lebanon. However the original curse will be lifted from Mount Zion and nothing will cause hurt or destruction there. In a sense, Mount Zion will be like the Garden of Eden as recorded in the book of Genesis (Ez.36:35). As in the time of Adam and Eve, the world was good and filled with God's bounty; however the Garden of Eden was especially blessed. In similar manner during Christ's physical reign upon this earth, the world will be blessed to a limited extent, whereas Mount Zion will be an **especially blessed** place. The fruit of the trees will be multiplied as will the produce of the fields (Ez.36:30).

> **"'Behold days are coming,' declares the Lord,**
> **'When the ploughman will overtake the reaper**
> **and the treader of grapes him who sows seed;**
> **when the mountains will drip sweet wine and**
> **all the hills will be dissolved,'"** Amos 9:13.

The animals that dwell on the Mountain of the Lord will become tame, and little children will play with them. Nothing will cause hurt or pain here for it will be a place blessed of the Lord.

> **"And the wolf will dwell with the lamb, and**
> **the leopard will lie down with the young goat,**
> **and the calf and the young lion and the fatling**
> **together; and a little boy will lead them. Also**
> **the cow and the bear will graze, their young**

> will lie down together, and the lion will eat
> straw like the ox. The nursing child will play
> by the hole of the cobra, and the weaned child
> will put his hand on the viper's den. They will
> not hurt or destroy in all My holy mountain,
> for the earth will be full of the knowledge of
> the Lord as the waters cover the sea," Is.11:6-9.

The magnificence of Mount Zion will be difficult to articulate. Isaiah chapter 60 and verses 1 to 3 states that darkness will be over the earth and deep darkness over the peoples, but the Lord will rise upon us and His glory will appear upon us. Nations and kings will come to see this great sight, bringing the wealth of the nations as an offering with them. This will be the occasion of the great 'end-time's wealth transfer' (Pr.13:22 & Ecc.2:26), not something we will do in the dispensation we live in, but it will be the Lord's doing as Jesus Christ sits on the throne of David and the obedience of the nations is His.

Forget about New York, London, Shanghai, or Moscow; Mount Zion and the holy city Jerusalem will be at the centre of the world (Ez.38:12) and the peoples of the earth will look to it for their supply and direction. Those who have musical ability at that time will sing,

"All my springs of joy are in you," Ps.87:7.

Following the judgement of His people before the bema of Christ, the Lord will create a canopy over the whole of Mount Zion and her assemblies that will be spectacular to see and will mark it out for miles around.

> **"Then the Lord will create over the whole area
> of Mount Zion and over her assemblies a cloud
> by day, even smoke, and the brightness of a
> flaming fire by night; for over all the glory will
> be a canopy. There will be a shelter to give
> shade from the heat by day, and refuge and
> protection from the storm and the rain,"** Is.4:5-6.

Some of the mortals who dwell in the earth at this time will have the privilege of living in the holy city along with the sons of God. Though still mortal, it appears that their natural life will be extended due to living in such a blessed place (Is.65:20, Is.66:20-21, Jer.3:14).

Psalm 48 speaks much of the coming beauty and splendour of Zion. It speaks of the holy mountain, "Beautiful in elevation, the joy of the whole earth…the city of the great King." In verses 4 to 6 the Psalm speaks of kings assembling together and passing by seeing this great sight. It says that they are amazed, are terrified and they flee in alarm. It is almost as if they are coming to Mount Zion in order to attack it, to wrest back control of the kingdoms of this world from the One who now sits enthroned and who rules over the nations (Ps.47:8). However once they see the magnificence and grandeur of Mount Zion, His dwelling place, a great panic seizes them and they become as weak and helpless as a woman in childbirth. They do not even attempt an attack because they know it would be doomed to failure. It would be a futile exercise; they flee away.

> **"Walk about Zion and go around her; count her towers; consider her ramparts; go through her palaces, that you may tell it to the next generation. For such is God, our God forever and ever; He will guide us until death,"**
> Ps.48:12-14.

In the palaces of Zion the royal bride, the remnant church of God will bow before her Lord and be clothed in the finest of gold. Many will seek her favour and shower her with gifts, and her offspring will be princes throughout the earth (Ps.45:9-17). Truly the first will be last and the last will be first (Mk.10:31).

Administering the Kingdom

The Kingdom of Christ will last 1,000 years and will be characterised by justice, righteousness, peace and prosperity.

Amazingly there will be those who choose to resist the rule of Jesus and He will deal with these wicked people during this time, until all enemies are put under His feet. This process of forceful subjection may well go on at different times throughout the 1,000 years, but will always result in the triumph of Christ and His ministers.

> **"For as in Adam all die, so also in Christ all will be made alive. But each in his own order: Christ the first fruits, after that those who are Christ's at His coming, then comes the end, when He hands over the Kingdom to the God and Father, when He has abolished all rule and all authority and power. For He must reign until He has put all His enemies under His feet. The last enemy that will be abolished is death…..When all things are subjected to Him, then the Son Himself also will be subjected to the One who subjected all things to Him, so that God may be all in all,"** I Cor.15:22-28.

All implements for war will be made obsolete and instead used for useful purposes; armies will be disbanded and who knows if they will need police forces as the nations dwell in a peace and security such has not been known in the history of mankind. The immortals will teach the Word of the Lord to the people of the earth and this will become the standard for education, law-making and general conduct (Jer.3:15). With no stumbling blocks allowed nor a devil to tempt them, **righteousness will become the prevailing culture of the times.**

A warning is given in Psalm 2 verses 10 to 12 to those mortals put in charge of the nations of the earth during the time of Christ's millennial Kingdom:

> **"Now therefore, O kings, show discernment; take warning, O judges of the earth. Worship the Lord with reverence and rejoice with**

trembling. Do homage to the Son, that He not
become angry, and you perish in the way, for
His wrath may soon be kindled. How blessed
are all who take refuge in Him!"

The Rebellion

Amazingly at the end of the 1,000 years as Satan is released from
his prison, a great rebellion will break out against Jesus and His
people. Spurning the blessed experience of the last millennia,
mankind will return to type and show his true colours. It is
almost as if the Lord is showing us that even if man had a
millennium of peace, prosperity and security sheltering under
Christ's wings, we would eventually rebel against Him and put
self first because that is all the old creation is good for.

The specifics of this rebellion are recorded in Ezekiel chapters
38 and 39 as mankind en-masse turn against their Christ at
Mount Zion seeking to attack a land which is restored from the
sword, of unwalled villages whose inhabitants have been
gathered from many nations to the mountains of Israel, who live
securely with no bars or gates and who have acquired cattle and
goods who live at the centre of the earth (Ez.38:8-12). Though
the attacking army will be like a cloud, covering the breadth of
the earth and surrounding Jerusalem (Rev.20:9), its demise will
be sudden, severe and absolute, as it is written in Ezekiel 38
verses 22 and 23:

> "With pestilence and with blood I will enter
> into judgement with him; and I will rain on
> him and on his troops, and on the many
> peoples who are with him, a torrential rain,
> with hailstones, fire and brimstone. I will
> magnify Myself, sanctify Myself, and make
> Myself known in the sight of many nations;
> and they will know that I am the Lord."

The Great White Throne

The final judgement takes place here as all who were not brought before the judgement seat of Christ are finally called to account. All are judged according to what is written in the records of heaven and according to what they have done. No-one escapes this justice which is final and lasts forever. Anyone whose name is not found in the Book of Life is cast into the lake of fire which is the second death (Rev.20:11-15). The awfulness of this place cannot be described but is just deserts for those who willingly reject the riches of His grace expressed in the sacrifice of Jesus on the cross. The holiness of God will not allow sin to go unpunished, and the **penalty is so grave because the gift of salvation in Jesus was so costly.**

New Heavens and a New Earth

Following this last judgement, the Lord will create new heavens and a new earth. The curse will finally be removed from **all** creation and there will be no more death, mourning, crying or pain as the old order of things will have passed away (Rev.21:1-5). All evildoers will be receiving their just deserts in the lake of fire, but the righteous will dwell with Him who is holy. God will live with His people, never to be separated again; the water of life will be freely available to all God's children. There will be no need for the sun to shine as the Lord God will illumine everything and night - time will be abolished.

Chapter 7
A Summary

I began chapter 2 listing questions I wished to answer in this book. Was the Kingdom going to be something spiritual or physical? Are we supposed to take it by force now, taking cities and nations for Jesus or will this happen at His return? Is it something that only has relevance now, or will it just be seen in the future? What about Jerusalem or Mount Zion and the 1,000 year reign of Christ; and what about the Kingdom parables and their particular perspective? And finally in view of these things, what is the gospel of the Kingdom all about?

Rather than focus on favourite scriptures that back up a popular viewpoint, I have tried to take an overview of **many** scriptures to gain a **comprehensive picture** of what the Word of God points to overall. This is why I have quoted so many scriptures in this book, verses that are often ignored when looking at things from a particular angle. I feel we will usually miss what God wants to speak to us if we are not willing to change our doctrinal viewpoint when we come across verses that do not match up with our pre-conceived ideas. This may be a humbling experience but is critical to gaining a **full understanding** of what the Word of God is actually saying. Also I have sought to establish what the early disciples believed about the Kingdom and what they were expecting rather than what 21st century Christianity is expecting in these days.

I believe it is clear that the Kingdom has powerful relevance today, but is only seen in its **fullness** once Jesus returns. There is an aspect of Kingdom rule that we can see today through the authority of the Holy Spirit working through believer's lives, and indeed it is incumbent upon us to learn to walk in this power as His Spirit leads us. However this is but a **small foretaste** of what is coming with the return of the Lord Jesus. Presently we have the Kingdom **coming**, not the Kingdom come.

When Jesus Christ does eventually return, He is coming to receive His Kingdom and take up the seat of power, namely the throne of David. This is the Kingdom come in all its fullness. He will rule from Mount Zion located in geographic Israel of today which will become the centre of the world's commerce, power and worship. As indicated in most of the Kingdom parables, at Christ's coming He will gather His servants to His judgement seat to divide the true servants from the false, the sheep from the goats. This will be on the basis of what they have **done**, whether they have the **evidence** of an alive or dead faith. Those who have kept the faith to the end, who are worthy to stand before Him will receive immortal bodies and inherit the Kingdom of their Lord. Those who are found to be false will be cast away into the eternal fire prepared for the devil and his angels. At this time grace will be poured out upon the ethnic Jews who have survived and they will fall at Christ's feet and acknowledge Jesus as their true Messiah. The natural branches will be grafted back into their own olive tree (Rom.11:24).

The immortals will administer the Kingdom, reigning with Christ for a thousand years as He puts all enemies under His feet. They will be His kings and priests and through them Christ will rule the nations with a rod of iron. The law will go forth from Zion and righteousness, justice and truth will become the **prevailing culture** of the times. Though Satan will provoke the nations to rebel once the thousand years are through, this rebellion will be put down in the fires of judgement and the final reckoning will take place before the Great White Throne. All those whose names are not found in the Lamb's Book of Life will then be thrown into the lake of fire.

The gospel of the Kingdom is primarily the message of the return of Jesus and the separation that will happen at His coming. To preach this gospel is to focus on the establishing of this Kingdom, as Jesus sits on the throne of David and judges the household of God dividing the wheat from the tares, the good fish from the bad, the sheep from the goats. If this message is preached correctly to the whole world as Jesus said it should be, as a testimony to them, the true church will get herself ready for the appearing of her bridegroom. This is the gospel of the Kingdom the world and indeed those who would walk on the narrow way that leads to life, must hear loud and clear. The bride will then be ready, without spot or wrinkle or any other blemish and finally it will be time for the end to come, the consummation of the age, the Kingdom come!

Chapter 8
Will You Inherit the Kingdom?

What other question can be quite so important for us to ask ourselves as this one, yet how many of us ever do? I believe the reason for this could be two-fold. Firstly we often don't see the need, as we've probably already been told we're saved by the person who helped us to 'become a Christian'; hence why should we even consider such weighty matters? Secondly whether we realise it or not, we are often so taken up with the things of this world that the call of the Spirit within our hearts becomes so faint we barely hear it. The still small voice is drowned out by the urgent demands of an unsatisfied flesh and the circumstances and busyness of life that so easily dominate our attention instead. This is a constant danger, especially relevant in the fast-paced modern societies in which many of us live, where the constant noise of people, advertising, media and indeed life itself attacks us incessantly.

What Perspective Do You Have on Life?
In Luke 16 verse 16 Jesus made this statement:

> **"The Law and the Prophets were proclaimed until John; since that time the gospel of the Kingdom of God has been preached, and everyone is forcing his way into it."**

When the gospel of the Kingdom is preached as it was in Jesus's day, a **conviction** comes upon those who hear it. It is a gospel that shows us how **perilous our state** is unless we are truly disciples of Jesus. It's like being on the Titanic enjoying a stroll down the concourse without a care in the world, looking forward to and planning for our new life in America. We have on our best clothes; we mix with important people and have a great future ahead of us. All of a sudden there is a tremendous noise and the captain's voice ordering everyone to abandon ship - we've hit an iceberg and will sink in minutes! All thoughts of our rosy life in America, the land of the free vanish in an instant as our minds are concentrated on finding one of the few lifeboats that will save us from a dreadful watery grave. Our fine clothes and possessions now mean little to us as we feel the boat sinking and struggle to force our way into one of these little craft that are our only means of escape. Decorum and elegance goes out of the window as **life preservation** takes over. This is what it is like when we hear the gospel of the Kingdom. Our perspectives change and we focus on what is important instead. We do **whatever it takes** to 'force our way' into the Kingdom of God.

Those Who are Led by the Spirit are the True Sons of God
I hope I have made it clear that just because a person has prayed the sinner's prayer or has come to the faith in some other way in their life does not automatically entitle them to a place in Christ's Kingdom. Jesus is looking for those who fight the good fight, who hold on to faith with a clear conscience (I Tim.1:18-19), who undergo sanctification by the work of the Holy Spirit (I Thess.4:1-8) and who actually have evidence of a genuine, alive faith at the bema of Christ (Jam.2:17-26). The scripture says that only those who are putting to death the deeds of the body by the Spirit of God are the ones who are being led by the Holy Spirit of God. Only these individuals are the true sons of God (Rom.8:12-14). **Those who do not follow the leading of the Holy Spirit on a consistent basis are not the children of God. It's as simple as that.** Those who live according to the flesh will die whether or not they have prayed the sinner's prayer, been baptised, been a part of a Christian family or not missed a Sunday service for the past 50 years.

God is looking for those who have **walked** according to the Holy Spirit, have **lived** by faith and have the **good deeds** to back up this claim once He returns. A good tree will only produce good fruit whereas a bad tree will only produce that which is rotten. God will be looking to see if we have the good deeds to evidence a faith walk. And these are not good deeds we do in order to try and get saved, but good deeds that **naturally flow** from a person who is dominated by the Holy Spirit. If you find it easy to walk in sin you are not being led by the Holy Spirit but the spirit of this world. The spirit a person has is the part of their being that motivates and compels them in life. It is the unseen force that drives their attitude and resultant actions. This I why it is easy to see who the children of God are and who are the children of the devil. He who **practices** righteousness is of God because he is **led** by the Spirit of God, whereas he who practices sin is of the devil (I John 3:9-10). Only a person who is led by the Spirit of Holiness can accurately call themselves a 'new creation in Christ.' How many of those who attend church today, who believe they will make it into heaven are not new creations at all but just a glossed up pseudo - spiritual version of the old creation?

But What if I Sin - Have I Blown it?

Of course this does not mean we never sin or stumble in the faith. I John chapter 1 and verse 8 says,

> **"If we say that we have no sin, we are deceiving ourselves and the truth is not in us."**

We must aim for perfection but unfortunately we have not yet got there! We all stumble and fall. Not one of us can say with confidence that we will never fall into sin again. However sinning should not be a regular, continuous habit otherwise repentance has no meaning to us as to repent is to **turn away** from the sin and go in the **opposite direction**. How can we say we repent for the same sins day after day when there is no evidence of us turning away from them? How can we watch pornographic images on a daily basis, habitually view women with dirty eyes or regularly slander those in the body of Christ and think we're okay because we asked Jesus to forgive us every day? How can we **practice** sin on a daily basis and then just say, "Dear Lord please forgive me"? Is there any repentance here, or are we just walking in sin and trying to put a spiritual plaster over it?

> **"For if we go on sinning WILFULLY after receiving the knowledge of the truth** (talking to church people), **there no longer remains a sacrifice for sins, but a terrifying expectation of judgement and the fury of a fire which will consume the adversaries. Anyone who has set aside the Law of Moses dies without mercy on the testimony of two or three witnesses. How much severer punishment do you think he will deserve who has trampled underfoot the Son of God, and has regarded as unclean the blood of the covenant by which he was sanctified, and has insulted the Spirit of grace? For we know Him who said, 'Vengeance is Mine, I will repay.' And again, 'The Lord will judge His people.' It is a terrifying thing to fall into the hands of the living God,"** Heb.10:26-31.

Technically speaking we could say that Jesus will forgive all who come to Him because He is a God of love. However He has put the condition of **repentance** before forgiveness. The number one priority to walking in the faith as a Christian is repentance. It is the first foundation of the faith listed in Hebrews chapter 6 and verse 1, coming **before** the foundation of, "Faith in God." Every one of Christ's apostles demanded repentance as the precursor to walking in faith, yet we seem to think this does not really matter as long as we say we are repenting from our sins when we ask for forgiveness. This is so wrong yet seems to be a very popular view of Christianity especially in the West as it does not require a change in our lifestyles. Many church goers today by practicing this modern view of 'Christianity' are deceiving themselves that they are headed for heaven, when actually they are on the broad road that leads to destruction and don't even realise it.

Striving Against Sin?

The one who is led by the Spirit but who falls in a trespass will immediately feel the awful conviction of sin in their spirit and seek to truly repent of it. This is a **normal state of affairs** for a true believer. They **cannot tolerate** nor live with sin in their lives. In Hebrews chapter 12 and verse 4 the writer talks of believers striving against sin, a struggle that could even go to the point of shedding their own blood. How many of us could honestly say we strive against sin in our daily lives? How many of us actually have a **strategy** for overcoming sinful habits in our lives, or have we swallowed the new 'wisdom' that states we should not focus on sin and repentance because this is negative thinking? If we have a penchant for cutting people down with our words do we focus and work on how we speak and force ourselves to converse gracefully; and when we fall back into old habits do we deal with our pride and apologise as a matter of priority? Or if we have had a problem with lust and pornography, how wise is it to have our own computer that is password protected preventing anybody from seeing what we are doing in private? To strive against sin, should we not do all we can to be **accountable** and **transparent** even if it is awkward and means other people can see what we are doing online, including on any social networking site? We could say similar things about alcohol and drug abuse, theft or lying. What **practical strategies** do we have in life to help us **overcome** these sinful traits and weaknesses we all have in our lives?

Now it is clear that we should not be so focused on sin that all we do is wallow in our weaknesses and inadequacies and lose sight of the immense gift of grace that has been given to us in our Lord Jesus Christ. However if we never feel the **disgusting effect** of sin in our lives we will never be motivated to be free of it. Instead it will continue to dominate our minds, just we will not realise this because we have become so used to living with it. This is a very dangerous place to be in life.

What we also need to realise is that an unwillingness to deal with sin is in reality a vote to keep walking in it. Until we have got to that place in life where we have put off the old man and put on the Lord Jesus Christ and become complete in Him, we will always struggle with sin and its effects. Passively walking through life with no strategy in place to deliberately put off the old man (which is still dominated by the flesh), will lead to a type of **carnal Christianity** which in reality will save nobody. All true believers must go through a period of striving against sin if they are ever to mortify the deeds of the flesh and put on the new man which in God has been created in righteousness and holiness of the truth (Eph.4:17-24).

Additionally we need to realise that we are literally at war with the prevailing culture of our times. The cultural environment we live in is constantly attacking and undermining our sanctification and faith walk with the Lord. In a sense we cannot help being spiritually defiled by the world due to the level of corruption and increase in wickedness all around us. However there is a lot we can do to prevent **unnecessary** contaminations from defiling us by watching what we do and where we go. If we are used to visiting nightclubs or spend long hours watching late night TV on our own, it should not be surprising that we do not feel the presence of the Holy Spirit as closely as we once did. By disciplining ourselves for the sake of being holy we will prevent ourselves drifting into a brand of Christianity that is friends with the world but is the enemy of God. Such Christianity will be useless on the Day of Judgement.

Holy Armour

Ephesians 6 is the famous chapter detailing the armour every believer is supposed to be wearing that they may fight the good fight of the faith. The apostle Paul exhorts us to,

> **"Put on the full armour of God, so that you
> will be able to stand firm against the schemes
> of the devil,"** Eph.6:11.

Because there is a fight we are involved with, a deadly struggle between light and darkness, it is **imperative** we are found clothed in the correct spiritual armour. Looking at the kit we are supposed to be wearing, it appears most of it is defensive whereas only one item, the sword of the Spirit can be classed as offensive. Why is this? If a person is a true believer, they are **already in** a victorious position over the enemy because they are, "In Him," who won the victory over sin and Satan. They do not need to try and fight the devil; the devil is already defeated! Why fight and try and duel with an opponent who is already beaten? The fact is the fight we are in is all about **walking** in the righteousness, faith, truth, peace and salvation Christ has **already** provided for us in Himself. It is walking through life righteously by the power of the Holy Spirit and thereby, "Putting on the breastplate of righteousness." It is **walking in the truth** and thereby, "Girding our loins with truth." It is **resting by faith** in the love of God and **walking faithful to Him** in life that shows we have, "Taken up the shield of faith with which we can extinguish all the flaming arrows of the evil one." Striving and warring against sin in our lives by the power of the Holy Spirit (and **not** by futile acts of penance or self-abasement) is **true** spiritual warfare. Overcoming the lusts of the flesh by actively following the leading of the Holy Spirit and standing in this state of purity and holiness may not sound as dynamic and exciting as fighting against demons and devils, but this is the type of spiritual warfare we are called to engage in.

I believe in deliverance, but much of the so-called 'spiritual warfare' that is undertaken today is nothing less than a futile exercise in self-delusion where people think they are pushing back the forces of evil but are actually wasting copious amount of time in futility. This includes the modern practices of 'warring in the heavenlies,' 'warring in tongues,' and 'duelling with demons.' If we come across an unclean spirit and the afflicted person desires deliverance and has repented of all known sin, then we can press ahead safe in the knowledge that Christ has given us power over the works of the enemy. However this 'fighting/duelling' style of spiritual warfare has its roots in a machoistic desire to look strong and a reliance on the arm of the flesh, rather than the power of the Spirit. Evil spirits are not 'cast down' due to the aggressively bold statements we make, nor the volume of noise we emit and not even from the ridiculous postures we go through when 'fighting' against these demons. They are cast out by someone who wears the full armour of God and is led by the Spirit of God.

True spiritual warfare is walking a sanctified life and preaching the true gospel. This is what all the apostles did and in so doing, saw the miraculous power of God released through their ministry. Not one time can you find any of the disciples of Jesus nor our Lord Himself ever engaging in these so-called 'spiritual warfare' techniques because they are unbiblical and a dangerous path to engaging in dead works rather than walking by faith in the Son of God. They took hold of the principles of Ephesians chapter 6 and learnt to be, "Strong in the Lord and in the strength of His might," (verse 10). They learnt to fight the good fight of the faith by standing firm in Him and in His righteousness, standing against the devil and his schemes through a position of strength. From this secure position they then **preached the true gospel**, using the sword of the Spirit to good effect. When the apostle Paul stood in the city of Athens, a place wholly given over to demonic idol worship, he did not start railing and praying against principalities and powers that were controlling the local population in a vain attempt to create an open heaven over the city. No, he stood in the righteousness of God and boldly preached the true gospel to those gathered there, a gospel message of repentance, faith in the true God, the resurrection of the dead and the coming judgement (Acts 17:16-34). By standing in the full armour of God and using the Sword of the Spirit to good effect, he reaped an eternal harvest of human souls.

The enemies of Israel could never defeat them so long as they walked in the holiness of their God. The only way they could wish to defeat Israel was by putting temptation before them and hoping they would fall for it. In this way their enemies hoped to provoke the wrath of God against them and indeed their evil plan was successful. This was the strategy of Balaam in the Old Testament (Num.31:16 & Rev.2:14) and is still Satan's way today.

There is a rest in Christ, but out of this rest comes a wrestling and striving against sin that marks out any true disciple of Jesus Christ. The two go together and result in a strong Christian witness, the victory of God and a blessed assurance on the inside, an inner conviction of a glorious future reality.

What about Eternal Security?

A number of you will have a hard time with what you are reading in this book as you've always been told that you're saved and that this is an 'eternal salvation'. In other words, once you've come to Jesus you can never lose that salvation; it is forever. The book of Hebrews tells us that Jesus paid the price for an, "Eternal redemption," (Heb.9:12), and that He is able to, "Save forever (or completely) those who draw near to God through Him," (Heb.7:25). This is a great comfort to us who have put our faith in Jesus and are walking with Him. However do these verses say we cannot lose our salvation once we pray the sinner's prayer, or once we truly come to the faith? Not at all.

In Hebrews 9 verse 12 the writer is showing us the eternal nature of the salvation Christ has purchased for us by His blood. He is showing that nothing more needs to be done - it is a completed work. When Jesus declared, "It is finished," He really meant it. Everything Christ accomplished on the cross is perfect; we cannot add to it and it is sufficient to, "Save us forever," so long as we also, "Draw near to God through Him," (Heb.7:25) and **remain** in that completed work. Whether we remain in that completed work, in the eternal redemption He has purchased for us is down to whether we remain in the faith or not and that is to a large extent down to us.

The scripture says very clearly that we are saved, "By grace, through faith," (Eph.2:8). The grace of God is His gift towards us; we cannot earn it nor do we deserve it. It is the gift of grace. In like manner faith is also a gift from God, something He gives to the objects of His grace (Rom.12:3). However it is incumbent upon us as recipients of this divine favour, to **walk in this grace and**

walk in this faith. If we do we are kept in that wonderful place of eternal security from which nobody or nothing can remove us. As it says in Romans 8 and verse 35,

"Who will separate us from the love of Christ?"

Remaining in the faith is the way to live in this secure position in Christ, confident of what is ahead. And this is not doing works in order to be saved, not at all! Remaining in faith entails maintaining the **rest of faith** within (Heb.4:3-11) by keeping a **clear conscience before God.** When we sin, the man of faith will immediately feel his conscience troubled and feel **compelled** to deal with that sin through confession and repentance. Committing the sin does not mean he stops walking by faith, but as his faith rest has now been troubled by a defiled conscience, he must now **deal** with that sin. A true disciple has no choice as he cannot live without that peace within, the true rest of faith in his heart. Isaiah 57 verse 21 says, "'There is no peace,' says my God, 'for the wicked.'" If we have sinned or cherished sin in our hearts we will not have that peace that comes from faith within us. This is a serious matter and indicates whether we are in the faith or not. Whether the believer chooses to deal with the sin or covers it up is his choice to make and will prove whether his faith is genuine or not. Dealing with the sin is not doing works to get saved but is walking by the Holy Spirit and living by the Spirit (Gal.5:25). This is **not an option** for a true follower of the Lord Jesus Christ.

Many today speak of the wonder of God's grace and how great it is to 'walk by grace.' However Titus 2 and verses 11 to 13 say this,

> **"For the grace of God has appeared, bringing salvation to all men, INSTRUCTING** ('teaching' - NKJV) **us to DENY ungodliness and worldly desires and to live sensibly, righteously and godly in the present age, looking for the blessed hope and appearing of the glory of our great God and Saviour, Christ Jesus."**

How can we say we are walking by grace if we are actively saying **yes** to ungodliness and worldly desires, are **not** living sensibly, righteously or Godly in the present age, and are **not** looking forward and anticipating the glorious return of our Lord Jesus? What grace do we think we are walking in because it is certainly not the grace spoken of in the Bible? God's kind of grace comes free of charge; but once it is received it will then **teach you** how to walk as a believer. Once again, this is not salvation by works, but walking in the true grace of God, not the fluffy, emotionally driven, self-pleasing 'grace' we too often speak of today but the, "Amazing grace...that saved a wretch like me...**grace that taught my heart to fear**, and grace my fears relieved." Is this the grace you are walking in or have you taken hold of the pseudo-grace that many people cling to today, a 'grace' that will be worthless on the day of judgement. The true grace of God is something that is living and effectual within. This was the grace the apostle Paul walked in, a dynamic **force of grace** he wrote about in I Cor.15:10,

> **"But by the grace of God I am what I am, and His grace toward me did not prove vain; but I laboured even more than all of them, yet not I, but the grace of God with me."**

Is this the type of grace you have operating in your life? If you are a true believer it should be.

Chapter 9
The Normal Christian Life

True Christianity is a lifestyle of walking with a Holy God, of maintaining faith in Him come what may. It is the pursuit of knowing God and being known by Him, of being found in Him a fruitful branch that abides in the vine, a true house that is established upon good foundations upon the Rock which is Jesus Christ. It is having the roots of our faith based on the six foundations of the true faith given in Hebrews 6 verses 1 and 2. These are,

> **"Repentance from dead works...faith toward
> God...instruction about washings** (baptisms)
> **and laying on of hands, and the resurrection of
> the dead and eternal judgement."**

These six foundations are **crucial** to the development of any Christian's life. They are called the 'milk of the Word' (Heb.5:12-14) and are as important to any new believer as a mother's milk is to a new-born baby. We would not think to deprive a baby of its milk; such an evil person would probably be imprisoned for a baby cannot survive without this source of nourishment. Yet how many baby Christians are being fed a diet of everything **but** the foundations of the faith? Without milk a baby will die; without spiritual milk the baby Christian will die too - it is inevitable. If a person does not have a reasonable grasp of the foundations of the faith, it is difficult to see how they could ever grow up to truly know God and be known by Him. The foundations of their life are not being laid upon the sure foundation of the Rock which is Jesus Christ. And if we are being honest, how many people who consider themselves believers today, even preachers may I add, really have no firm concept or grasp of what these foundations truly are? Far too many we would have to say.

Not everyone begins the journey in the same way. We should not insist that people have to follow our formula in order to get saved. However there is a Biblical standard of what characterises a true believer and what does not, and if we look at what the Bible means by a Christian we will come to understand that this is far away from the definition many people give it today.

What we need to realise is that not everyone who thinks they are a Christian truly is, and many who **assume** they are because 'they always have been' or because they 'prayed a prayer' are not disciples at all but like the Pharisees are whitewashed tombs that on the outside look great but on the inside are full of dead men's bones. A Christian is one who is 'Christ-like,' who walks in step with a holy God and is quick to deal with sin should they fall into it. Those who walk in wilful, unrepentant sin cannot call themselves Christian (Heb.10:26-31, I John 3:4-10); after all to repent from dead works is the very first foundation of the faith and if we can't even walk in repentance what foundation is our life based upon? Certainly not the foundation which is the Rock Christ Jesus. Those who also **trust** in dead works and thereby fall from grace cannot call themselves Christian either (Gal.5:4). Likewise people who have their faith in another gospel and another Jesus (Matt.7:24-27), those who are no longer salt and light in their community (Matt.5:13), those who bear bad fruit in their lives (Matt.7:16-20, John 15:1-6) and individuals who do not do the will of the Father and who do not know Him can neither call themselves a Christian (Matt.7:21-23) according to a Biblical perspective. Add to this those who hate their own brethren (I John 2:9-11), those who engage in unrepentant idolatry, immorality, testing the Lord and ungodly grumbling (I Cor.10:1-12), and they who are unwilling to carry their own cross (Lk.14:27) and you get a long list of people who disqualify themselves from bearing the name Christian. We could go on but I hope you get the point.

How to Fill the Church With Goats and Tares.

Unfortunately today we tend to label someone a Christian as fast as we can, perhaps so they don't turn around and change their minds before we've got them settled in our churches! Many who respond to altar calls and pray the sinner's prayer today have no idea of what it means to be a true believer and would probably not come forward if they really did know what they are signing up for (Lk.14:25-35). One of the reasons for this is the gospel we have all too often presented to people is one which says, "Come to Jesus and get saved. Once you're 'saved' we don't have to talk about salvation anymore because it all happened when you got 'born-again'. You have everything you're going to get of 'salvation' so now it's all about getting others into our church, getting them 'saved' and having a great life together!" This is a modern Westernised view of Christianity which emphasises bigger and bigger churches, a church growth model we are successfully exporting all over the Christian world with our dynamic media. The end result is that we ruin whole communities of what were once genuine indigenous believers who have instead been seduced by our hype and consumer-driven easy gospel. You can see it taking root everywhere, from Africa to the Far East, often spread by local leaders who seek to emulate the lifestyles of money and influence being paraded before them by the proponents of this modern Western form of 'Christianity'. What such local leaders often end up doing is just stuffing the church full of tares and goats, with people who equate Christianity with a **superficial emotional experience** they get at the 'new breed' type of church. They could not be further from the truth.

Just yesterday I was listening to a preacher declare how he had prophesied that there would be a million salvations in one meeting, an event that happened recently at a huge crusade in Africa. Now I am all for crusades and reaching as many people as possible. Let the evangelists get out there and preach the good news! However this preacher then made a big thing about the fact that one million people got '**saved**' at this meeting and would therefore be going to heaven (inferring of course that it had all happened because he had prophesied it in the first place). This is not the truth, though it appeals to our instant success, numbers counting brand of 'Christianity' that is so prevalent today, especially in charismatic circles. It is great to see a million people respond to the gospel, praise God! But which gospel did they respond to? Was it the heart convicting message that compels a person to kneel at the cross in repentance in order to be free from sin, or the, "Come to Jesus and He'll give you a new life," type of message that is technically accurate up to a point but does not really deal with man's hardened heart? How many of these million souls who signed those decision cards were actually born-again that day? And if we just assume that a large number were, how many of them will fight the good fight of the faith, persevering to the end so as to be truly saved? I would love to think that all of them would but in reality judging by experience I believe the real number will be a lot less.

Radical Changes.

True Christianity is not all about experience. However to say we have literally passed from death to life and that the Spirit of the Lord God Almighty, the Creator of the universe now dwells within us which is what we are saying if we claim to be 'saved', there should be some sort of reaction within us! When something was dead and now is alive again, there is a **huge difference**. A starker contrast could not and does not exist. Though Christianity is not about experience per se, I would have to question whether someone has truly been saved if there is no **radical change** in their lives as a result of their conversion experience. The Holy Spirit is a **force** of life and holiness that simply **energises** and **compels** us to righteous living. The Bible is very clear that only those who have the Spirit truly belong to Christ (Rom.8:9-10) and what is different about these individuals is that their spirits are **ALIVE** because of righteousness! As it says in John 1 verse 12:

> **"But as many as received Him, to them gave**
> **He power** ('ability, privilege, force, right,
> capacity' - Strong's concordance) **to become the**

**sons of God, even to them that believe on His
Name," (KJV).**

If someone has become a new creation in Christ they will know
it. They possess the very force of life itself, the very nature of the
Divine Being Himself hidden in their fragile human frame. So
many of those today who are told they're 'saved' because they
mouthed some words and prayed a prayer are deceiving
themselves. Jesus said that the gate is small and the way is narrow
that leads to life, and there are **few** who find it (Matt.7:14). He
also said,

> **"Strive** (literal Greek - 'agonise') **to enter
> through the narrow door; for many, I tell you,
> will seek to enter and will not be able,"**
> Lk.13:24.

There are many people seeking to enter the Kingdom in these
days. The question is, are they actually making it through the
door and if they have not yet truly entered, why are we telling
them that they have? And when their soul still cries out for the
living waters that they have yet to experience do we tell them,
"Just focus on these scriptures that tell you that you are saved.
They should comfort you and sooth your conscience." Are we
helping these people or just feeding them a false, hollow gospel?
So often we tell people, "Come to Jesus, He's got a great plan for
your life!" Technically speaking this is true. God does have a
great plan for our lives; He wishes good for His children as any
father would. However this is only **part** of the truth. To take hold
of the blessing, we first need to turn our backs on the old sinful
life (repentance) and learn to be disciplined by the Lord and walk
in step with the Holy Spirit. I can understand there are
individuals out there who have been through systemic abuse,
neglect and mistreatment who will respond positively to the hope
offered in the statement, "God's got a great plan for your life,"
and they probably do need to hear it. However they also need to
hear a message that will lead them to deal with their own sin that
is so often obscured by the trauma they have been through. We

are all desperate sinners who must learn to come to the cross in complete helplessness before a holy God, and throw ourselves at His mercy in order to find that 'Amazing Grace' that opens wide the gate of salvation before us. Only a **personal brokenness** will result in the **immense glory** of the love of God being poured out **full measure** in our lives!

I have also heard people say, "When you're catching fish, you must bait the line, catch them and then clean them up by gutting them. You don't try and gut a fish before you've caught it!" The message is that we shouldn't try and change people before we 'hook' them into the Kingdom. We need to get them in first by baiting the line with something they want, and once we've got them we then clean them up. There is again a truth to this point of view; we are called to be fishers of men, to catch people in the net of the Kingdom of God and people need to come to God before He will begin the process of sanctification in them. However the inference is then made that we should not mention sin, righteousness or the coming judgement when reaching out to people with the gospel because that would be trying to clean the fish before we've caught it and what we need to do is hook them in with something attractive that they will like. Mentioning negative things such as sin and judgement is considered the 'old religious way' which needs to be replaced with the 'new way' of attracting people into church with nice looking bait. Certainly we should not put a stumbling block in anyone's way if they are searching for God, nor be deliberately offensive to show how 'old school' we really are! However the bait that God expects us to put on the hook is the **promise of freedom** from sin, the world and the flesh, the **glorious reality** of a clean, holy life, free from guilt or condemnation, not a lure that appeals directly to our flesh! Unfortunately most people won't find the bait of holiness too attractive unless they first hear the true gospel message, the **gospel of the Kingdom.** Once they hear this message and the Holy Spirit begins moving in their hearts, they will be crying out for the bait of holiness and a clean heart. No-one will be able to stop them forcing their way through the narrow gate and into the Kingdom.

And then there is the journey. We are required to maintain and walk in the faith once for all handed down to us. There is a small gate but there is also a narrow way that leads to life and many have the tendency to stray from the path. There can be many reasons why this occurs but I feel one of the main ones is the fact that too many people don't even realise they can wander from the path and even if they did they do not know what can cause such a diversion. We often know so much about our favourite sports team or reality TV show contestant yet have almost zero knowledge of how to walk out a successful faith life. This is a tragedy and is causing untold harm in the body of Christ. As it says in Hosea 4 and verse 6:

> **"My people are destroyed for lack of knowledge."**

This is one of the main reasons I am writing this book. That hopefully I can help people to see the reality of their Christian life, where they are going and whether they are on the narrow path that leads to life or on the broad road that leads to destruction and did not even realise it.

How many of those who sit in our pews have at some point departed from or denied the faith but do not realise what has happened because they were taught such a thing could not happen? All they have is a shallow, spiritless Christianity that is devoid of life, power and assurance yet they have no way out because **they think** they are a true believer.

The Pilgrim's Progress.

One of the greatest and probably the most influential book of English literature ever written is the classic, "Pilgrim's Progress," penned by the renowned Christian author John Bunyan in 1678. If this writer had ever set eyes on what is considered 'Christianity' today, I doubt very much whether he would have recognised it as such, in view of what he wrote in this book. It details the story of 'Christian,' the man who finds a Bible and after reading it falls under the **conviction of sin** represented by a heavy sack tied to his back. This sack is bulky, heavy and burdensome and however he tries, Christian just cannot shake it off. It perfectly illustrates the way our soul becomes burdened by its load of sin once the light of the Holy Spirit starts to shine into our darkened hearts. The conviction is so strong that he eventually runs away from his own home in the city of destruction and begins the long journey through many pitfalls, difficulties and dangers to the Celestial City. After much struggle with the heavy weight of conviction still weighing him down, he makes it through the Slough of Despond where he almost gives up. He then takes a risky diversion at the town of Morality where the people trust in their own righteousness and meets characters such as 'Backslider' trapped in his cage of despair, 'Unready' terrified by dreams of judgement day, and the stern looking soldier who almost loses his life fighting his way through to the door that leads to the Kingdom; this is all **before** he ever gets to enter through salvation's door. He is undergoing a **process** of wrestling within, whereby his heart is being **prepared** to wholeheartedly turn his back on the old life, to truly repent and throw himself on the mercies and grace of God Almighty. This process may be diverse for different people depending on how open and ready their heart is. Nevertheless we must allow God to lead us through this process before we will be ready to truly enter through the door of salvation. In a sense we can enter through the door at any time; the day we live in is called the, "Day of Salvation," (II Cor.6:2). However our hearts are all too often hardened by the deceitfulness of sin and usually we are so blinkered to the fact that God has to do a **thorough work** in us **before we are ready** to truly enter through that door that brings such overwhelming joy to our hearts.

Christian eventually finds grace at the cross where he is released from his heavy load of sin. He has striven and agonised to get through the door of salvation that many try to enter and do not manage (Lk.13:24). How different to our user-friendly, "Come to Jesus, He's got a great plan for your life!" type of Christianity that promises the world yet results in emptiness and **zero assurance** of salvation. How different is the overwhelming joy and freedom experienced by Christian compared to the fleeting goose-bumps, hyped up emotionalism and no real change that too many feel today when they are told they are 'saved' by leaders who should know better. After much striving, Christian is finally freed from his conviction of sin and makes it through the door of salvation, an event that propels and motivates him to make it through the stiff challenges ahead. Jesus said there is a narrow door and few find their way through it. If you have made it through, **you will know it;** it will be obvious to you and to those around you. Darkness has become light and death has been resurrected to new life. The contrast cannot be any clearer.

Once Christian finds grace at the cross and makes it through the narrow gate, he continues his pilgrimage to the Celestial City. His first task is to make it up the Hill of Difficulty, past the ferocious lions and to the Palace Beautiful. From here he walks straight into a pitched battle with Apollyon who showers him with burning arrows and almost deals Christian a fatal blow. As if this is not enough, he has then to navigate his way through the Valley of the Shadow of Death complete with deep darkness, flames, billowing smoke, traps, pitfalls and fierce creatures. Vanity Fair comes next where Christian and his new-found friend Faithful are imprisoned, chained, beaten and put on trial before Lord Hategood and his twelve vicious jurymen who condemn Faithful to death. Christian manages to escape and continues along the King's Highway, the narrow road that leads to the Heavenly City. As it becomes steeper and more difficult to traverse, Christian and his new friend Hope see an easier road over the fence and take a slight detour along By-Path Meadow, a path **they are told** will take them to the Heavenly City. Unfortunately they have been **lied to** and find themselves prisoners of Giant Despair locked up in Doubting Castle. After much suffering at the hands of this giant whose mission in life is to knock all hope out of believers, they miraculously escape and run as fast as their legs will carry them back to the King's Highway. They learn the hard lesson that pilgrims must **keep to the narrow way** come what may in order to make it through to the Celestial City.

Through further trials and beautiful places they travel, meeting many along the way. Some of these are true believers such as Goodwill, Evangelist, Watchful and Sincere who encourage and aid their Christian brethren. Others are fellow pilgrims who have turned back from journeying to the Heavenly City through one reason or another, usually down to character weaknesses they exhibit represented by their names such as Pliable, Timorous and Mistrust. Still others are individuals set on turning Christian from the narrow path such as Worldly Wiseman, Obstinate, Greedy Gehazi and Talkative. Occasionally he comes across fearful sights such as the precipice known as the 'Hill of Error' unsuspecting pilgrims had fallen down after straying from the path, or the huge black hole called the 'By-Way to Hell' those who lie and cheat and sell their souls for money fall into. Eventually through more adversity and trying times punctuated with times of refreshing and rest, Christian and Hope finally make it through to their ultimate goal, the Heavenly City. It is a happy ending for our heroes but an altogether different prospect for those who did not keep to the King's Highway, the narrow path that leads to life (Matt.7:14). They do not make it to the great City; they are lost forever.

The author John Bunyan obviously believed it took more than just a quick prayer or a general inclination to be forgiven of our sins to get us through the narrow gate, to 'get saved.' It took the light of God's Word shining into a darkened, sinful heart that prompted a **deep conviction** in the person's heart, a conviction that could not be placated nor ignored, a conviction only the grace of God can appease. It took a **rending of the heart**, a striving to do business with a holy God, a laying down of the old life in order to take hold of the new life in Christ. And equally Bunyan understood it required **ongoing** humility, faith and perseverance for a pilgrim to make it through to the Heavenly City. Those who never take a hold of their salvation or those who just drift through life will find eventually that they are not walking on the King's Highway but by then it may be too late to do anything about it. No doubt he wrote the story as a warning to believers to **guard** their hearts, **maintain** their walk of faith and to take these matters extremely **seriously**. By portraying these perhaps sombre issues via an easy to understand story, he hoped to reach as many as possible with a message that would destroy every vestige of **complacency** in the minds of his hearers and replace it instead with a sense of **urgency**, a compelling desire to do **whatever it takes** to be like Christian and make it to the City of the Great King.

All through the story you get the distinct impression that to John Bunyan, normal Christianity started with a **defining conversion experience** and was then a **daily walk** of resisting the flesh and learning to walk by the Holy Spirit. At any time we could be diverted from the path either by the fear of man, the seduction of the enemy or by walking according to the desires of our flesh. If this should happen as it did to Christian when he stepped off the path, it may not necessarily mean we have departed from the faith; however if we continue walking away from the path, we will not make it into heaven. Only those who, "Endure to the end," (Matt.24:13) will be saved, not those who only make it halfway. The key issue for Bunyan was whether a person had truly got saved, and if they had truly become born-again, how were they living their life in order to **stay** in this secure position. As long as Christian stayed on the King's Highway and kept moving forward, nothing could stop him from reaching the Celestial City. The whole issue was whether he **stayed** on the narrow way and **never gave up** whatever the devil or the world threw at him. And if he found that he had wandered from the path, was he prepared to do **whatever it took** to get himself back onto the narrow way? This is authentic Christianity, a 'fight of faith' (I Tim.6:12) that results in the salvation of our souls; it is the only type of Christianity that matters in the long run.

True Christianity is a faith walk, and the important thing is to determine which path we are walking on, who we are walking with and which direction we are going. When a child is learning to walk it takes time and they will often fall over. However as they persevere, they fall over less and less till eventually they learn to walk and even run, skip and jump! Similarly as we get born-again, we are like little babies needing to grow up. As we attempt to walk by faith we will inevitably fall over and hurt ourselves. This is normal. If we are diligent and continue on a good diet of, "The pure milk of the Word," (I Pet.2:2) and get up every time we take a tumble, **continuing** in the faith, eventually we will learn to walk by faith and can even go on to do great exploits for our God! The Bible exhorts us not to remain as infants but to **grow up** in our salvation (I Cor.13:11). How many believers today have been walking around with dummies in their mouths for the last 15 or 20 years of 'being a Christian' but have never yet learnt to get off all fours and walk like a mature person should? It's time to put childish ways behind us and grow up in our salvation.

Is Christ Formed in You?

In Galatians 4 and verse 19 the apostle Paul says,

> **"My children, with whom I am again in labour until Christ is formed in you…"**

Speaking to his children, those who had come to the faith, he is perplexed about them and their faith walk, making the observation that Christ was not yet formed in them and he desperately wanted this to happen. Verses like this one just don't compute with our modern view of the gospel. How can one be saved yet not have Christ formed in them? If you're saved, don't you have Christ in you? As I have already mentioned, many people today who think they are saved are actually not at all. They may have had some sort of emotional experience or even felt a touch from the Lord yet never made it through the narrow gate. These people have no chance of Christ being formed in them because they have not yet come to Him by entering the gate which is Him (John 10:9). Then there are the ones who have been born again but like little babies left with no nourishment they have faded away. They never managed to grow because there was no nourishment to aid that growth, and what spiritual life there was got extinguished within them. Then there are the ones who through the taking of offence, being seduced by the flesh or through the bright lights of this world are caused to stumble in their faith walk.

The whole aim of our Christian life is to, "No longer to be children…but…to grow up in all aspects into Him who is the head, even Christ," (Eph.4:14-15) to become, "Complete in Christ," (Col.1:28) to have, "Christ…dwell in your hearts through faith," (Eph.3:17) to have, "Christ…formed in you," (Gal.4:19) to, "Put on the new self which in the likeness of God has been created in righteousness and holiness of the truth," (Eph.4:24). This is a **state of being** we as believers are to aspire to and work towards. It is a state of being in which we are at one with Him in our hearts, consumed by the very presence, glory and love of Christ, founded on the foundations, full of an alive faith and the sure and steadfast hope that anchors the soul and results in that blessed assurance within! **This is true Christianity!** Such a thing does not automatically happen when we 'get saved'. A young baby is not the 'mature man' we are supposed to be. He has still to get weaned, learn to walk, talk and feed himself, grapple with getting an education, deal with puberty, learn accountability and respect, stand on his own two feet, take responsibility for his wife and family, train his children in a Godly manner and set an example those around him will aspire to.

Getting born again is the **first step** on the journey towards the ultimate goal of attaining to the measure of the stature which belongs to the fullness of Christ. Along the way a baby Christian first needs to be fed on the pure milk of the Word, to become **established** in the foundations of our Christian faith (Heb.6:1-2). Once this process is complete and only then can he be weaned onto the stronger meat of the Word, the deep mysteries of the faith. As he begins to grow breathing the oxygen of the life-giving Spirit, feeding on the heavenly manna, drinking deeply from the living water poured out from heaven, he learns to get off all fours and to walk by faith. He may stumble many times along the way but all he does is get up again through repentance, dust himself off by sanctifying himself to God and keeps walking by faith looking straight ahead unto Jesus the author and perfecter of his faith (Heb.12:2).

As he walks by faith he educates himself in the Word, learns accountability and respect within the household of God and learns to stand by faith through the trials and difficulties he encounters along the way. As he wrestles with mortifying the deeds of the flesh and overcoming sin in his life (Rom.6:11-14), he truly learns to fully **take hold** of the grace and love that have been poured out upon him (Rom.5:2) and he enters the rest of faith. As he enters this rest and confidence in Jesus we can start to see that Christ is being formed in him (Gal.4:19). Christ is now dwelling in his heart through faith (Eph.3:17). He has learnt to lay off the old man, has been renewed in the spirit of his mind and has put on the new man which in the likeness of God has been created in righteousness and holiness of the truth (Eph.4:22-24). The rest he enjoys and the hope of heaven that is now so real to him secures his heart like an anchor that is strong enough to keep him in the storms of life (Heb.6:19). It naturally results in the **full assurance of faith** within (Heb.10:22), what we often call the 'blessed assurance.' This is that divine confidence and security in the reality of our future inheritance in Christ's Kingdom, the conviction that one day soon we will live and reign with Jesus when He comes to establish His rule on this earth. This blessed assurance dwells in our hearts and acts as the **evidence** of coming glory. And this is not the end! As he learns to walk and be established (Rom.16:25) in this rest of faith and becomes a mature believer and has the assurance of faith within, the ultimate goal is to become, "**Complete in Christ,**" (Col.1:28). This is what the apostle Paul was referring to when he said he had not yet attained it but pressed on to take hold of that for which Christ Jesus took hold of him (Phil.3:12). No doubt Christ was being formed in his heart and he had entered into the rest of faith. However he knew there was still more and he reached out for it with every ounce of his being.

The apostle Paul spoke of 'running the race to win,' (I Cor.9:24) of disciplining his body so that he would not be disqualified but would achieve the imperishable crown. If this is how Paul viewed things, why are we telling people they are the done deal once they've prayed the sinner's prayer? This is not a Biblical perspective! It is another gospel.

126

Christianity is the pursuit of the high calling we have received in Christ Jesus. It is the drive to,

> **"Attain to the unity of the faith, and of the
> knowledge of the Son of God, to a mature
> man, to the measure of the stature which
> belongs to the fullness of Christ,"** Eph.4:13.

The apostle Paul did not consider himself yet to have attained this blessed position in Philippians 3 and verse 12 but pressed on to lay hold of that for which also he was laid hold of by Christ Jesus. He exhorted all who were perfect, that is those who are truly saved and walking in step with the Holy Spirit, to follow his model of Christianity and pursue the high calling of God with every ounce of their being.

> **"Brethren, I do not regard myself as having
> laid hold of it yet; but one thing I do:
> forgetting what lies behind and reaching
> forward to what lies ahead, I press on towards
> the goal for the prize of the upward call of God
> in Christ Jesus** (the regathering/snatching away
> and resurrection of those who are found 'in
> Him' at Christ's second coming). **Let us
> therefore, as many as are perfect, have this
> attitude,"** Phil.3:13-15.

Paul gave us his example and exhorted us to follow it, to have the same attitude. Goodness only knows what he would have made of the easy-fix, formulaic, consumer-driven 'Christianity' so many of us have invented and are following in these days! And his reaction will be nothing as to the reaction that Jesus Christ will give it at His coming of this we can be sure.

The parable of the sower gives us an easy to understand view of this exact process at work, showing how the different people react in different ways. Some seem to make a decision for God, but their hearts are so hard the new creation never has a chance to even take root in them and they are not changed (Mark 4:4). They are like those where the seed fell beside the path. Other people come to the faith and then hit a sticky patch in life which causes them to fall away quickly. The soil of their hearts was not deep enough to allow the new creation to grow and it withered and died (Mark 4:6). The plant started growing but the individual's heart could not sustain the growth. Too many rocks inhibited its development. These are like those where the seed is sown on the rocky ground. Still others have a **depth** to their hearts, they have the **potential** to be a new creation in Christ, but they are distracted by the things of this world and the growth in their hearts is eventually snuffed out as over time, the thorns grow up and choke the life out of it (Mark 4:7). There was life there alright, only it never produced anything of value. In due course the life was squeezed out of it by the thorns. They are unfruitful and as such are cut off from the vine and put to the side. In the end they will be burned (John 15:6).

> **"Every tree that does not bear good fruit is cut
> down and thrown into the fire,"** Matt.7:19.

Many people thought these individuals were great Christians because they seemed to have new life in them and indeed they once did. Unfortunately however the snares and pitfalls of life described by Jesus in the parable of the sower manage to kill the new creation that was formerly growing in their hearts, because they were not diligent in rooting out the thorns as Jesus instructed them to. A good plant is one that grows up and produces fruit. The test of a true believer is do they continue in the faith even when things get tough, and do they persevere so as to produce fruit in due season? Only such people can accurately call themselves a **true Christian**.

The Blessed Assurance.

It is my conviction that every true believer in the Lord Jesus Christ should have the blessed assurance within as their **standard Christian experience**. For some reason we have made it a by-product, a 'nice if you've got it but don't worry if you haven't' sort of experience. I believe this is wrong. The scriptures say:

"Let us draw near with a sincere heart in full assurance of faith, having our hearts sprinkled clean from an evil conscience and our bodies washed with pure water," Heb.10:22.

Many people today talk of having a 'honeymoon experience' when they first come to faith in Christ. They suddenly feel clean on the inside and close to God. It is a wonderful time but eventually wears off as the realities of life in a cursed and fallen world grind down upon them. The impression is given that this is normal and we may perhaps feel this closeness again, but only very rarely if at all. People crave the exhilarating sense of being close to the Living God again and many go in search for it but not that many seem to get established in it as a **normal** part of their Christian faith walk. Some search for it again in pursuing good deeds; others look for it in hyped-up, dynamic and contemporary emotionally-driven worship services. There can be all manner of ways we try and experience it again yet how many of us can honestly say with hand on heart that the blessed or full assurance of faith is a **normal** part of our Christian lives? Certainly in the Western world I believe it is very few.

I am convinced both through the study of God's Word and my own personal experience that there is a level or intensity of Christian living that very few people seem to know about today. I've heard so many people sing about being a new creation yet how many truly are something completely different, in fact the **opposite** of what they once were? How many have undergone the upheaval of a radical transformation in their lives which now makes them a **new** creation, old things being passed away and **everything** being new (II Cor.5:17)? How many in the church today are **utterly different** to the person they once were through knowing Jesus Christ, and how many are really just the same as they always have been only they now possess a 'holy' veneer covering their supposed Christianity? How many have become a new man in Christ, or do we just aimlessly sing about these things thinking that this description applies to everyone in the church?

In my experience I have rarely come across anyone who accurately articulates these **essential processes of Christian growth** with **understanding** and **personal insight**. How many preachers today have truly entered the rest of faith, have become established in Christ themselves and are a completely new creation, a mature man in Christ? No doubt such leaders exist but how many compared to the number who would not be able to give a coherent answer if questioned about these critical phases of spiritual development? If the leaders have not experienced these stages of Christian growth themselves and often don't even realise the importance of them, how can they ever lead anyone else to experience them? It is an impossibility. A person can never lead anyone to a place they have never been to themselves. There is an **URGENT** need today for leaders in God's church who have truly experienced this genuine growth in Christ to arise and start leading others to experience it too. People's eternal destiny depends on it.

The goal of every believer is to become established in the faith, to put on the new man or the new self, to be made complete in Christ, to be found in Him. The Bible paints a very clear picture of the process everyone called to follow Jesus must undergo, a progression from being a child in the faith to becoming mature and founded or established in Christ. This process is given different names in scripture such as the, 'Fight of faith,' (I Tim.6:12), 'Abiding in the vine,' (John 15:4), 'Walking in the light,' (I John 1:7), 'Running the race,' (I Cor.9:24) or, 'Working out your salvation with fear and trembling,' (Phil.2:12). The end goal of this process is to become, "Complete in Christ," (Col.1:28), that is to be so shaped and moulded by our faith walk with the Holy Spirit that our old self no longer lives in our body but has been crucified and killed off completely, only to be replaced by the **new creation** which is **in Christ**. We have allowed the Holy Spirit to break us and indeed put us to death that our sole or **dominant**

identity is now the new us which is connected and **fused to Christ**, as the apostle Paul put it,

> **"It is no longer I who live, but Christ lives in me; and the life which I now live in the flesh I live by faith in the Son of God, who loved me and gave Himself up for me,"** Gal.2:20.

As we come to this place of maturity in our Christian walk, after struggling and striving against sin, we enter the glorious **rest of faith**, the position of being at rest from our struggles because we now know our identity is to be found in the new creation in Christ. We literally are a new creation in Christ, old things are gone behold all things are new! We are **secure** in our salvation not by trying to convince ourselves through holding particular doctrinal positions, but through fighting the great fight of faith, taking hold of the eternal life to which we were called and having the living hope birthed in our hearts by the Holy Spirit. Being at rest in God leads directly to the blessed full assurance of faith within; the joy and peace of God become rooted in our hearts. This wonderful state of being has been entered by many good believers down the centuries and the Lord is still calling His people to **pursue and enter it today**.

Personal Experiences.

I came to faith in 1984 after a long period of resisting the call of God. The problem was I knew that if I became a Christian my life would have to change and I did not want that. I was 16 years old and the bright lights of this world drew me very strongly. I had been brought up in church from day one and had sensed the distinct call of God on a number of occasions, even telling people that one day I would be a church minister (I was in the Baptist church at the time). However I had never quite come to that point of turning my back on the world and living wholeheartedly for Jesus; and the longer I left it, the more the conviction of God would grow within my heart! I knew if I died I would go straight to hell and I really didn't want this. Finally my heart could take no more and I surrendered my will to that of my Heavenly Father. Joy flooded my heart and I felt like I was a new person; the choice had been made, the die had been cast and I was thrilled to be experiencing a supernatural sense of life deep in my heart. I was literally walking on air!

I had finally made the choice to live for God and I was really going to do it. I felt washed and clean and released from the awful weight I had been carrying about with me. It was my bona-fide 'honeymoon experience.' I immediately had a desire to work for the Lord and told people I was going to be a missionary. All my priorities changed; I had a strong desire to read the Word of God, even I admit to the detriment of getting to school on time or doing the things I really ought to have been getting on with!

Over the years as a Christian 'radical' I attended every meeting going, from Baptist to Pentecostal, Anglican to charismatic house church. In time I felt myself drawn to the 'Faith Prosperity' movement and embraced its teachings wholeheartedly, eventually giving up everything to attend one of its Bible Schools in Uppsala, Sweden. This is where I met my wife Tanya, a lady who had grown up within the Pentecostal church in Communist Bulgaria. She was one of the first believers in that country to escape the Communist system which held all in its iron grip, and make it to a Bible School in the West. Somehow all on her own as a young 18 year old she made it by train across Eastern Europe and slipped into Denmark and then Sweden under the very noses of the Communist authorities!

Once we were married we looked forward to a life serving God together. We became partners with all the major 'faith' ministries, sowing financial seeds wherever possible. I would constantly listen to preaching by these ministers in order to build up my faith so that the supernatural power of God could be released in my life. I was careful to maintain a positive confession at all times to obtain healing and to achieve success. In time I began investing in the stock market, using my own money and my faith techniques to increase financially. At first I started making easy money; I boasted about setting up a Christian hedge fund and looked forward to earning my first million. I was a prosperous, successful man of God! My positive confessions were working to increase the value of my shares, or so I thought.

Then disaster happened. The dot-com bubble broke and I was horribly exposed to the tune of thousands of pounds. I desperately fought on, thinking the devil was attacking me and all I had to do was truly get 'into faith' and speak my way to success. We were in a church which taught us to 'never quit; God will make you successful, He loves you so much,' so this is what I did. After taking quite a financial hammering, I took to really seeking God as to which stock I should invest in. I thought this was a good strategy to employ to 'spiritually' get me out of the hole I was in so this is what I did. I distinctly remember feeling led to invest in one technology company at a time when I had already lost most of our money and it was really make or break time. This was it. I felt God had told me to invest so I leveraged myself out and 'stepped out in faith' as we were constantly encouraged to do. After all if you 'had faith' you should act on it, so that is what I did. The next morning the very same company had issued a profit warning and its share price dropped by 40%! I was completely wiped out and plunged into debt. It was such a shocking thing to happen, my heart dropped like a stone. It was gripped by fear and anguish inside. If you have ever had such a thing happen to you, you will know what I mean. What added to the sense of hopelessness and frustration was that it felt that **God had personally led me into financial ruin**. It was like God Almighty Himself was **fighting against me**. Such a thing just did not compute with my 'Faith-Prosperity' brain; I could not understand what was going on.

The storms of life had really hit and my whole family was taking a battering. I had lost a six figure sum that was a **monumental** loss to someone in our situation in life, a knock that still affects us today. However the knock it gave to the Christianity I believed in and held dear to my heart was even greater. I had done everything I was supposed to do; I had even put my 'money where my mouth was' as we say in the UK and lost all of it. Why had God led me into this and why did He not deliver me when I was in my hour of greatest need? Why had he 'set me up' so to speak in that last trade that completely finished off all my hopes and dreams? Why had He plunged me into relative poverty when I was supposed to be His child; is that what a good father does? Why, why, why?

Probably one of the smallest yet most significant events of my life happened at that point of crisis. As thoughts I could not answer constantly weighed on my mind, feelings of Divine injustice weighed me down. However, instead of blaming God for what had happened I began to **praise Him anyway** despite the circumstances that shouted at me to do otherwise. I did not understand anything of what was happening; none of it computed. However I knew that God was good and He had His reasons though I was at a loss to understand them.

Over the months that followed I did not get any immediate answers to the questions that swirled around in my head. I **wrestled** with my faith and the principles I held to. I started **examining** the things I was being taught and sought to know whether they were of God or not. I remember considering what faith actually was and as my mind considered these things I came to see that at its essence, **faith was a rest**, a total reliance upon and trust in God Himself and what He had accomplished through Jesus Christ on the cross of Calvary. I suddenly realised all along I had been trying to **do things** to get more faith, to build up my faith, to walk in faith, rather than focus on the important issue which was **did I know Him whom my faith was supposed to be in**? It occurred to me that all my positive confessions, all my breakthrough offerings, all my giving to get was just dead works dressed up as Christianity. I had been straining to perfect what I was **doing**, in order to really be a man of faith. Now I realised that I had not been building a faith in anything but in my own 'faith.' My focus was not on Him who was supposed to be the **object** of my faith, the One whom my faith was supposed to be in, but I had been focusing all the time on building 'my faith.' I had not been at peace or at rest in Him, but was constantly striving to **get** that faith, to make things happen by 'my faith'! I had developed a Christianity of dead works and **did not even realise it**. Like Christian in Pilgrim's Progress I had wandered from the King's Highway by people who had told me it was the way to the Heavenly City. I had been wandering down a pathway of dead works 'Christianity' that in the end would not have led me to Christ's Kingdom.

As I understood these things an **amazing peace** flooded into my soul, a peace I had not felt for many a year in 'active Christian service.' For sure over the years I had on occasion felt blessed and touched by God. I had known times of feeling good on the inside. But this was not a state of being I experienced **daily**, an **integral part** of my everyday existence. It was very occasional and usually only happened after I really tried hard to reach out to God in worship or did something extra-spiritual. If I were honest I could not always say I felt saved. But this was different; I felt I had truly **entered into** the peace of God and the rest that came from a living faith in Him. I felt a great weight lift from my shoulders as I realised that faith was not something I had to build and work for, but a **gift of grace** that would naturally grow the more I came to **know God** and Jesus Christ His Son. **Knowing God** was the important issue; was I resting in Him or was I wrestling in my own strength? All of a sudden I realised I had been reading the Bible through 'Faith/Prosperity' tinted glasses. This false gospel had become the **prism** through which I viewed all the scriptures and without realising it I had become a slave to a system of religion that promised much but was a one-way ticket to self-righteousness, disaster and ultimate separation from God. It was a frightening thought! I looked around me at the other people I knew still stuck in this empty religion of men and felt grave concern for them. The only reason I had come to know the truth was because I had taken the message I was hearing to its logical conclusion and been burnt severely. This experience had **compelled** me to question the principles I had been taught and had made me realise that I was on the wrong road and needed to do **whatever it took** to get back on the narrow road that led to life. But what about the others who had not gone to such lengths but were wandering aimlessly down this broad road that leads to destruction and didn't even realise it? How could they see they had left the narrow way and had been deceived into following the lie of the serpent?

I suppose a natural question that springs to mind at such a time is, "If I had died when I was still following this Faith/Prosperity religion of dead works, would I have gone to heaven?" I knew that I had been born-again in 1984 that was certain. Yet I had inadvertently wandered from the path and had begun to trust in another Jesus and another God. If I am honest I felt a sense of fear as the enormity of what had happened and the ease at which I had fallen for this lie of the enemy shook me. I had always considered that I was a pretty good Christian when I compared myself with those around me. I knew quite a bit of the Bible and was an active church member on many fronts. I even preached in church and in our Bible School! Now I realised I was as gullible as the next man and was completely at the mercy of a Sovereign God to take the blinkers from my eyes. It was all down to His mercy and His grace, and the only way I could access that was by maintaining a humble heart before Him. What a hard lesson that was to learn!

I could not accurately answer the question posed in my mind and I suppose it is a technicality as the Lord in His mercy did not allow me to continue along this broad path that leads to destruction. However I have no doubt that if I had not been diverted from my march down this road, I would be standing on His left at the judgement seat of Christ gnashing my teeth with all the others and crying out along with them, "Lord, Lord, did we not prophesy in Your name, and in Your name cast out demons," (Matt.7:22) wondering how on earth I had been so easily deceived to end up shut out of the heavenly Kingdom. How many people are out there walking a similar path, **completely oblivious** to the fact that they have **wandered from the path** and are no longer walking in the full assurance of faith as they should be? As I consider these things I have a tremendous burden and indeed foreboding of what lies ahead for many in today's church who clearly think they are going to heaven but will one day find out they were on the wrong road all along.

By the grace of God I have finally begun to grow up in my faith and in the things of the Spirit. At first I started to become aware of my spirit man inside me, a new creation growing up within the tent of my body that **craved holiness** and the touch of God. As I nourished it by feeding on the Word of God I came to be more and more conscious of it and could tell when I had defiled it through sinful behaviour. Like a baby crying out for milk, my spirit man was craving the pure milk of the Word and I was compelled to feed it! I did not have to force myself to read the Word. No, it was the very thing I looked forward to doing. I remember sitting down to read the Bible and sensing my spirit man just anticipating the feast it was going to enjoy, exactly as a hungry man's appetite is stirred as he contemplates the scrumptious food before him just before digging in! There were times I would be working when the thought to read my Bible just popped into my mind. As I considered this thought, I immediately sensed the spiritual hunger pangs coming from the new creation within me that longed for the nourishment of God's living Word.

As I gave myself to the study of God's Word, I really lost a lot of interest in the things of this world such as the TV, newspapers and entertainment. The revelations of God's Word started coming one after the other and I slowly began to get a grip on what the Bible was all about and especially the foundations of the faith. As I gained new understanding of the mysteries of God in His Word it was like a **force of righteousness and life** was flowing in me and through me, blowing every negative and depressive thought and feeling out of me. A glorious flow of **Divine goodness** flooded over my soul. The apostle Paul exhorted all believers to, "Rejoice in the Lord always," (Phil.4:4); though previously difficult to do I now found it easy as the joy of the Lord coursed through my very being! I distinctly remember a number of times when I had been truly feeding on the Word, after I got up I would feel as though the holy fire of God was all over me and I was ablaze! It was an amazing experience. I felt if you could unzip me and see my new self within, looking past the outer flesh of the human body I live in, I would have been lit up with the very light and glory of God Himself.

As I grew, wrong things I used to be able to tolerate now became difficult to live with. Sins I used to be able to live with so to speak now became a major issue. If I committed a sin, I could not bear to live with it any longer. I had to deal with it or I felt myself wasting away within; and even after seeking God's forgiveness I would sometimes still feel the stain of its corrosive influence on my soul that was craving the righteousness of God, a defilement that affected me for a time. Committing sin became such a traumatic event that gradually I found myself walking free from it, certainly compared to how I used to live. The Bible says in I John 3:9,

> **"No-one who is born of God practices sin,**
> **because His seed abides in him; and he cannot**
> **sin, because he is born of God."**

This is not to say that I will never sin; I fully recognise that in and of myself that is in my old nature I am as eager to sin as the next man and unfortunately I am not yet fully separated from my old man. I still live in a body of sin that is corrupted and that one day I will have to set aside in favour of the new immortal body the Lord will give me on the great day when He comes again. However it is my experience that as I have grown in the Lord, the voice of the flesh has become less and less and the temptations of the enemy are not as compelling as they once were. As I have just mentioned, I still have every potential to sin and fall flat on my face, yet by the grace of God He is starting to form a hatred of sin in my heart through the new creation within me that is becoming **dominated** by the Holy Spirit. And one thing I know is that it is not easy to do something you hate doing! We need to have a holy hatred towards sin in our lives, not a passive acquiescence to it. Walking by the Holy Spirit and allowing God to build the new creation in our hearts will bring this about.

The reward of living and walking by the Spirit, of 'putting on the new man' over time, is the blessed **full assurance** of faith within that is the **evidence** of things to come. This is the place of **strength** for a true believer, the **quiet confidence** that you are **secure** in Him and ready to meet Him at His coming. It is the hidden rock of assurance within, the position of rest from which we then learn to walk in a manner pleasing to Him, the peace we have that guards our hearts and our minds in Christ Jesus. Believers who have this blessed assurance within have a **tremendous confidence** in their God, not a confidence in themselves but a deep-rooted confidence in the Rock Jesus Christ. Such confidence in God manifests itself as a **living faith** in our hearts, not a general belief that we believe in God, but an all-too real conviction that is the **evidence** of our salvation, the proof of what is coming, a faith that cannot be blunted, put out or thwarted, a conviction which is the, "Evidence of things not seen," (Heb.11:1-NKJV).

If I ask you the question, "How do you **know** you are a Christian?" I wonder what you would say. Would you refer back to the time you got born-again or got baptised? Both these experiences are important in our Christian walk and act as a reference point for us. However when we are talking about **knowing** you are a Christian we have to start thinking in terms of **evidence that demonstrates** this reality. If there is no evidence to back up your claim, how can you know you are saved? From a historic reference point in your life? What **evidence** do you have? As we have mentioned before, good deeds and a growing sanctification in your life is all good evidence to have. This shows you have been walking by the **Holy** Spirit. However what is probably the **most important** evidence of all is the blessed assurance within our hearts, that is the full assurance of faith that comes from a clean heart and conscience, an assurance that is a Divine gift from above, a faith that is a **rock-solid conviction** of things unseen. This is what we are talking about when we speak of the 'Blessed Assurance' not a fleeting feeling inside but a conviction and guarantee that if you stood before the judgement seat of Christ today, your sins would not stand against you but they will be gone forever. You know you will inherit the

Kingdom because you know the purity, holiness and glory of God in your heart that gives a **certain** confidence in your future. This is the full assurance of faith we all as believers need to possess.

A number of years back I was speaking to an experienced Baptist minister who had pastored for many years. He told me the **number one issue** Christians spoke to him more than anything else was the question, "What is the blessed assurance and how do I get it?" People understood they needed it but didn't really know what it was, whether they could have it and how this state of being could be accomplished in their lives. This is why I have taken the time to write from some of my personal story, both to try and articulate what I have learnt about the blessed assurance from my own experience and also how I came to walk in this blessed state. Not that I am trying to make out I've got it all sorted and I'm a perfect Christian, not at all! I just hope I can reach people with this critically important message before it is too late. By revealing some of the ups and downs of my own faith walk I really hope to demonstrate to all who are truly hungry to walk as a new creation, that the blessed assurance within is something that is **real** and is **available** to all who truly seek God with their whole heart and who never give up, despite what fires of refining He puts you through. God is no respecter of persons; however He will only work with individuals who are **humble and contrite of spirit** and who **tremble at His Word** (Is.66:2).

Chapter 10
Test Yourself

The apostle Paul says in Colossians chapter 1 and verses 22-23 that Jesus will present us before God holy, blameless and beyond reproach **if** we continue in the faith firmly established and steadfast, not moved away from the hope of the gospel. He also says to the Corinthian church that they would be saved as long as they **held fast** to the gospel message Paul preached to them, but if they did not they would have, "Believed in vain," (I Cor.15:1-2). The apostle John wrote in his second letter verses 8 and 9 that we should watch ourselves that we **do not lose** what we have accomplished but may receive a full reward. He says the one who does not abide in the teaching of Christ does not have God, but only the one who holds to the teaching does. Those who do not have God will not make it into the Kingdom of Heaven. They may have come to the faith at one time but they never **continued** in the faith so that over time, "Christ may be formed in them," (Gal.4:19). The plant was prevented from growing and eventually died. They were never made, "Complete in Christ," (Col.1:28), they never managed to enter the, "Rest of faith," (Heb.4:11). I could go on and on with scripture after scripture that warn us of these things yet how many of us when reading them actually realise what serious matters they are talking about? They are scriptures **directed at the church**, not to those on the outside.

Are You in the Faith?
In II Cor.13 and verse 5 the apostle Paul says to the church at Corinth,

> **"Test yourselves to see if you are in the faith;
> examine yourselves! Or do you not recognise**

> **this about yourselves, that Jesus Christ is in you**
> **- unless indeed you fail the test?"**

How many of us just **assume** we are in the faith because one day we prayed a prayer and someone told us we were saved? Or maybe we even got baptised so that surely settles it! One of the unwritten cardinal rules of preaching in the West seems to be that you never, ever dream of questioning whether someone is truly saved or not. This is just unacceptable because it may unsettle people and cause doubts to rise in their hearts regarding their Christian faith, and the one thing we want to do is help people to feel saved. After all if they feel saved they will be happy to come to our church and perhaps do Christian things like help in the children's ministry or with ushering, service which would be really helpful to us. So we avoid such questions at all costs and instead constantly seek to reassure people that God's got a great plan for their life and that they are on the road to heaven. If they don't feel like they are, we tell them they should find a scripture that sooths their conscience and helps them to feel saved again. The apostle Paul had a different approach. He told us (Christian people who are in church) to **examine ourselves** and see whether we are in the faith, to see whether we passed the test or not. Reading what Paul was saying in context, it seems that the test was whether you were walking in sin or were **overcoming** the lusts of the flesh (II Cor.12:20-13:7), whether you were living a repentant life or not. It is relatively easy to say we are walking with the Lord and to deceive others around us into thinking that we are, but one day we will be judged in righteousness and truth and nothing escapes the notice of the One who will judge us. As it says in Hebrews chapter 4 and verse 13:

> **"All things are open and laid bare to the eyes of**
> **Him with whom we have to do."**

Isn't This Talk of Judgement a Little Extreme?
I can imagine there will be those who read this book and think, "Isn't this all a bit extreme? I mean nobody I know talks like this.

Aren't we supposed to be enjoying life - didn't Jesus come to give us abundant life? Why all this seriousness and threat of judgement?" We have to realise that the culture we live in desensitises us to spiritual realities, especially in the West. Jesus often told the people around Him that they were spiritually **deaf and blind**, people may I add who were probably a lot more spiritually aware and Biblically literate than the average church-goer of today.

Jesus has come that we may have life and have it to the full; this is true enough. However this is **resurrection life** He is talking about, a force of life that comes through being disciplined by the Lord and maintaining our faith through this trial; a life that has known difficulties and the pain of loss, but through maintaining faith and a good attitude has then been comforted and strengthened by the love of God that has been lavished in their hearts by the Holy Spirit. He is certainly not talking of a vacuous, empty life that is all about shallow friendships, positive confessions, what stuff we have, how much money we make, and the fake images we present to those around us.

I have a friend who recently went through all the gospels to categorise the basic themes of Jesus's words and teachings verse by verse. His premise was that the things Jesus emphasised should be the things we emphasise, and the things which He spoke little of should likewise have less of a prominence in our preaching and teaching. Whilst not an exact science, what he found is sobering to say the least. Of the 1,874 verses researched, he found the largest proportion by some way at 29% fell into the category of, 'Warnings of Judgement,' 95% of which were directed to **His own disciples.** The second biggest category at 21% were words centring on the, 'Cost of Discipleship, Holiness and Obedience,' whereas one of the smallest categories at 9% was that of, 'Encouragement and Praise.' If he had also taken into account the words of Jesus spoken to the seven churches in the first three chapters of the book of Revelation, the category of, 'Warnings of Judgement,' would have been even higher. If approximately half of what Jesus spoke about centred on the so-called 'negative gospel,' that is warnings of judgement, the cost of discipleship, holiness and obedience, why does our preaching today not reflect this too? I ask you the question, how many sermons do we hear or books do we read today that really focus on the things Jesus did? Not many.

If you are a preacher today, what topics do you focus upon in your preaching? Are you warning the people as Jesus and His apostles did, or are you too concerned with unsettling folk that you just preach messages to tickle people's ears? Jesus is not looking for preachers who will just comfort the flock under their care, but He's looking for those who will reprove, rebuke and exhort with great patience and instruction (II Tim.4:2), not out of a spirit of 'lording it over the flock,' but out of love and **true compassion for their eternal souls**. God is looking for such preachers today, who will count the cost and preach the heart rending sin-convicting sermons that cause people to truly do business with God. They will probably not be popular and their books may not make it to the best-selling lists. But they will know an anointing from the Holy One and be people who know their God and see Him work mightily in and through them! They will have the very Word of the Lord in their mouth because they will be preaching the **Gospel of the Kingdom.** Will you be such a preacher? By God's grace you can be.

God put me into a wilderness experience far away from success and influence and started doing His work in me unseen from view. In the hidden place He revealed Himself to me and put a tremendous burden for His people in my heart. God is looking to and fro throughout the earth to find a people who will speak with a prophetic voice to this generation, who will prepare the way for the Lord and get His people ready to meet with their God. Are you prepared to go through **whatever it takes** to be this type of leader? The time is short and far too many virgins are curled up in bed snoozing, unready for their Master's coming and completely oblivious to their predicament. Are you prepared to disturb them in their slumber and waken them up? Only those who preach the Word as Jesus and His apostles did have a hope of reaching them. As the apostle Paul said to Timothy his son in the faith:

> **"I solemnly charge you in the presence of God and of Christ Jesus, who is to judge the living and the dead, and by His appearing and His Kingdom: PREACH THE WORD,"** II Tim.4:1-2.

Where Will You Be On That Great Day?

Brothers and sisters the time is so short. We are living in an age when the coming of the Lord is very near, the time when He comes to see who is truly His and who is not. Our Lord is coming for those who, "Eagerly await Him," (Heb.9:28) not those who take Him for granted and barely give His appearing a second thought. Jesus is looking for **overcomers** to share His Kingdom with, those who have been **faithful** in the things of this world, those who **walked** by the Holy Spirit, whose faith is alive and **proven** over time. He is looking for those He can entrust the future glorious Kingdom to.

When He comes the die will have been cast; there will be no second chances, it is the time for, "The Lord to judge His people," (Heb.10:30). The question is where will you be standing on that great day, on His right or on His left? Inside the wedding feast or locked out? With the Master as a part of His household, or thrown outside into the darkness where there is weeping and gnashing of teeth? The choice is yours. Brothers and sisters, I urge you to break up the fallow ground in your hearts, remove the thorns that so easily grow and choke your life within and humbly accept the Word of God into your heart, the Word that can save you. Turn off the TV, switch off the internet, leave the worldly magazines behind and get into God's Word as never before. The years of this life will pass you by in no time at all and then it will be the day of reckoning. Many on that day will look back at their empty, shallow, 'Christian' lives and regret over and over again their superficiality, their indifference to the things of God and the chances they spurned when they could have taken a different course in life but just let it pass through their fingers. Many who call themselves believers today have **no idea** of the responsibility they have before God and will waste their lives in **futile living** till it is too late and the decision for eternity is taken out of their hands for good.

The Choice is Yours

Beloved, it is not too late for you; you still live in the day of salvation, you still have opportunity to turn away from your secret sins and pursue the high calling you have received in Christ Jesus. If you have sin hidden in your heart, dark secrets that cast a shadow over your soul do not ignore them any longer. Some will need to confess sins to spouses or to a trusted friend; others may need to deal with unforgiveness and lay down grudges they have nurtured in their hearts for years. Letters may have to be written, phone calls made restitution given for stolen items. Whatever it takes to deal with sin and crucify its choking grip on our lives is a small price to pay for the glories that await those who walk in true holiness before Him. As it says in Hebrews 12 verse 14:

> **"Pursue peace with all men, and the sanctification** (holiness) **without which no one will see the Lord."**

And in I Cor.2:9:

> **"Things which eye has not seen and ear has not heard, and which have not entered the heart of man, all that God has prepared for those who love Him."**

Sin thrives in secret but its power is broken by openness, honesty and truth. This is what it means to walk in the light as He is in the light (I John 1:7).

Our Saviour commands us to give up all to be one of His disciples, to lay down our lives for the goal of knowing Him and loving His people. Those who find their lives in this life will lose them for all eternity, but those who learn to give up their rights and humble themselves under His mighty hand will find the life that is truly life! You have a high calling; not everyone will make it but the choice is yours. Nobody can make it for you. Jesus said,

> **"Seek first His Kingdom and His righteousness, and all these things will be added to you,"** (Matt.6:33).

Are you investing your life and efforts in building your inheritance in the coming Kingdom, or spending so much time building your kingdom here that you have lost sight of your heavenly calling? Brothers and sisters test yourself and see if you are in the faith. Be **honest** with yourself and with God. If you find that you don't have that blessed assurance in your heart that comes from a clear conscience and a faithful walk with Him, do not rest till you have established yourself in the faith once more! Repent from sin, not just with empty words but with **actions** and in **truth**. Throw yourself on the mercies of God and find the tremendous love and compassion of a Father who is willing to blot out the transgressions of those who walk humbly before Him. Find the peace of God that will guard your heart and mind in Christ Jesus as a living reality inside of you. This is the most important decision you can ever make-period. Don't waste another minute on futile empty living but start laying your treasure above, where Christ is seated at the right hand of God. As Jesus, John the Baptist and all the early disciples preached,

> **"Repent, for the Kingdom of Heaven is at hand,"** Matt.4:17.

My prayer for you is that as you seek Him with all your heart, you will find Him and enter the glorious rest of faith. I pray that you may have a clear conscience and a blessed assurance within that is the evidence of the things which are to come, the true conviction of an alive faith that will save us on that great day. As it is written in the book of Hebrews chapter 4 and verse 7,

> **"Today if you hear His voice, do not harden your hearts."**

May God's grace be with you as you seek to follow Him wholeheartedly, remembering the exhortation given to God's people in Hebrews chapter 10 verses 35 to 39,

> **"Therefore do not cast away your confidence** (your confident trust and faith in Jesus), **which has great reward. For you** (church people) **have need of endurance, so that after you have done the will of God, you may receive the promise: 'For yet a little while, and He who is coming will come and will not tarry. Now the just shall live by faith; but if anyone draws back, My soul has no pleasure in him.' But we are not of those who draw back to perdition, but of those who believe to the saving of the soul,"** (NKJV).

Will you be one who draws back from their faith and is lost forever in eternal destruction, or one who fights for and maintains their faith resulting in the salvation of their soul. The King is coming and His Kingdom is at hand; will you be ready to inherit it?

Lightning Source UK Ltd.
Milton Keynes UK
10 June 2010

155403UK00001B/80/P

9 780956 565402